D1629934

THE
ANGLER'S GUIDE TO
FRESHWATER FISH

Chris Turnbull 93

THE

ANGLER'S GUIDE TO FRESHWATER FISH

Habits and Characteristics
of over 50 British Fish

John Wilson and Chris Turnbull

BXTREE

First published in Great Britain in 1993 by Boxtree Limited

Text and Photographs © John Wilson 1993
Illustrations © Chris Turnbull 1993

The right of John Wilson to be identified as Author of this Work has been asserted by him in accordance with the Copyright, Designs and Patents Act 1988.

10 9 8 7 6 5 4 3 2 1

All rights reserved. Except for use in a review, no part of this book may be reproduced, stored in a retrieval system or transmitted in any form or by any means, electronic, mechanical, photocopying, recording or otherwise, without prior permission of Boxtree Ltd.

Edited by Helen Douglas-Cooper
Designed by Millions Design
Typeset by SX Composing Ltd, Rayleigh, Essex
Printed and bound in Great Britain by Butler and Tanner Ltd, Frome, for

Boxtree Limited
Broadwall House
21 Broadwall
London SE1 9PL

A CIP catalogue entry for this book is available from the British Library.

ISBN 1 85283 412 9

CONTENTS

Introduction	6
Cross sections of a river	7
Barbel *Barbus barbus*	10
Bleak *Alburnus alburnus*	14
Bream *Abramis brama*	16
Bream/rudd hybrid	19
Silver Bream *Blicca bjoerkna*	20
Bullhead *Cottus gobio*	22
Crucian Carp *Carassius carassius*	24
Crucian carp hybrids	26
Grass Carp *Ctenopharyngodon idella*	27
King Carp *Cyprinus carpio*	30
Coloured king carp variants	36
Wild Carp *Cyprinus carpio*	38
Charr *Salvelinus alpinus*	41
Channel Catfish *Ictalurus punctatus*	44
Wels Catfish *Silurus glanis*	46
Chub *Leuciscus cephalus*	50
Dace *Leuciscus leuciscus*	54

Eel
Anguilla anguilla   56

Flounder
Platichthys flesus   60

Goldfish
Carassius auratus   62

Grayling
Thymallus thymallus   64

Gudgeon
Gobio gobio   68

Stone Loach
Noemacheilus barbatulus   70

Minnow
Phoxinus phoxinus   71

Mullet
   Thin-Lipped Grey Mullet *(Liza ramada)*
   Thick-Lipped Grey Mullet *(Chelon labrosus)*
   Golden Grey Mullet *(Liza auratus)*   72

Golden Orfe
Leuciscus idus var. auratus   75

Perch
Perca fluviatilis   78

Pike
Esox lucius   82

Pumpkinseed
Lepomis gibbosus   86

Roach
Rutilus rutilus   88
   Roach/bream hybrid   92
   Roach/rudd hybrid   93

Rudd
Scardinius erythrophthalmus   94

Ruffe
Gymnocephalus cernua   97

Salmon
Salmo salar   98

Allis Shad
Alosa alosa   102

Twaite Shad
Alosa fallax   103

Smelt
Osmerus eperlanus   104

Three-Spined Stickleback
Gasterosteus aculeatus   105

Tench
Tinca tinca   106
   Golden Tench *(Tinca tinca var. auratus)*   109

American Brook Trout
Salvelinus fontinalis   110

Brown Trout
Salmo trutta   111
   Trout hybrids   114

Rainbow Trout
Salmo gairdneri   115

Sea Trout
Salmo trutta trutta   118

The Whitefish
   Powan *(Coregonus lavaretus)*
   Vendace *(Coregonus albula)*   122

Zander
Stizostedion lucioperca   125
   Walleye (Pike-perch)
   (Stizostedion vitreum)   128

INTRODUCTION

IN ADDITION TO COVERING EACH FISH'S HABITAT, its distribution, origin, reproductive cycle and feeding habits, and how to catch it, the purpose of this book is, of course, to identify positively each species (even the hybrids). This is done not by complicated scale and fin ray counts or by inspecting the creature's pharyngeal teeth (who wants to kill the fish in order to identify it?), but simply through artwork and photography. To this end we sincerely hope that together with concise text, the black outlines plus in situ paintings and close-up photographs, you will be able, in most cases, to put a name to the fish you catch.

We have not included certain species because either they are now rarely seen, or have actually become extinct. Take the burbot, for instance. Every species book currently available lists the burbot, yet no one has caught one anywhere in British freshwater for decades, possibly since the turn of the century. The burbot does, however, thrive in much of Europe, particularly in Scandinavia in the cold, clear, pure rivers and deep lakes, which as yet are still unaffected by pollution and farming fertilizers, unlike our British waterways. Pollution is the reason why certain species like the silver bream, bleak, and even the rudd are now becoming considerably less common than they once were. Quite simply, water quality has changed drastically in the twentieth century, greatly affecting the most delicate, vulnerable species, and unfortunately it will continue to do so.

John Wilson and Chris Turnbull
1993

Key to freshwater habitats (overleaf)

1 A lowland stream or brook Narrow, shallow and varying in current pace from stagnant to quite fast. Bankside vegetation and aquatic plants often most prolific.
Expected species: minnow, loach, bullhead, stickleback, eel, gudgeon, dace

2 An upper lowland river Can be sluggish or of a medium to fast pace, and varies enormously in depth. Usually rich in both bankside and aquatic vegetation.
Expected species: dace, roach, rudd, bream and hybrids, silver bream, bleak, perch, ruffe, pike, eel, zander, brown trout, grayling, barbel, chub, tench

3 A tidal lowland river Invariably wide, deep and affected by strong ebb and flood tides. Little aquatic vegetation.
Expected species: roach, bream, hybrids, perch, ruffe, pike, eels, gudgeon, chub, shad, flounder, smelt, mullet

4 An estate lake Man-made still water resulting from damming a stream at the bottom of a valley. Rich in nutrients from land run-off, with prolific aquatic vegetation.
Expected species: roach, rudd, bream, tench, perch, pike, eel, wild carp, king carp and coloured variants, catfish, golden orfe

5 A pond Small, natural or man-made still water of up to an acre or two in size, sometimes with dense beds of lilies, or broad-leaved potomogeton covering the surface.
Expected species: roach, rudd, crucian carp, bream, perch, pike, eel, catfish, pumpkinseed, golden orfe, goldfish, wild carp, king carp and coloured variants, grass carp, silver bream, tench, golden tench

6 A broad (tidal-river linked) such as the Norfolk Broads, which are in fact flooded peat diggings of the 13th century. Depth varies from 3-12 feet (1-3 metres) and the banks are lined with reed and alder carr.
Expected species: roach, rudd, bream and hybrids, tench, perch, ruffe, pike, eel, flounder

7 A gravel pit A man-made excavation resulting from the removal of mineral deposits laid down along river systems during the last ice age. Varying in surface area between 1 and over 100 acres (4,000-400,000m^2, flooded gravel pits are irregularly shaped with enormous variation in depth and plant life.
Expected species; roach, rudd, bream, silver bream and hybrids, tench, perch, pike, eel, zander, grass carp, crucian carp, king carp and coloured variants, rainbow trout, brown trout, triploid trout, American brook trout, hybrid trout

8 A mountain stream Swift, cool-flowing, shallow, often very rocky with minimal plant life.
Expected species: bullhead, loach, grayling, brown trout, sea trout, salmon, eel

9 A mountain pool Small, cool stillwater, usually stream-fed. Little aquatic vegetation.
Expected species: whitefish, charr, brown trout, sea trout, eel, salmon

10 Large mountain lake/loch/lough Sometimes in excess of 50-100 feet (15-30 metres) deep with vegetation only around marginal shallows.
Expected species: perch, pike, charr, whitefish, eel, sea trout, brown trout, salmon, occasionally roach, bream

11 An upland spate river Cool, fast-flowing, often with waterfalls and rocky pools. Vegetation generally only along margins.
Expected species: eel, sea trout, brown trout, salmon

12 A tidal spate river Often wide with both shallow stretches and deep holding pools.
Expected species: dace, roach, perch, chub, shad, brown trout, sea trout, salmon, eel

13 Man-made reservoir Result of damming a steep-sided valley for the purpose of both commercial and domestic water retention. Deep water rich in nutrients from farmland run-off. Massive phyto and zooplankton populations.
Expected species: brown trout, rainbow trout, eel, perch, pike, catfish, roach, rudd, bream and hybrids, tench, stickleback, king carp

14 An estuary River at the end of its life where it widens to pour its waters into the sea.
Expected species: eel, flounder, smelt, shad, mullet, sea trout, salmon

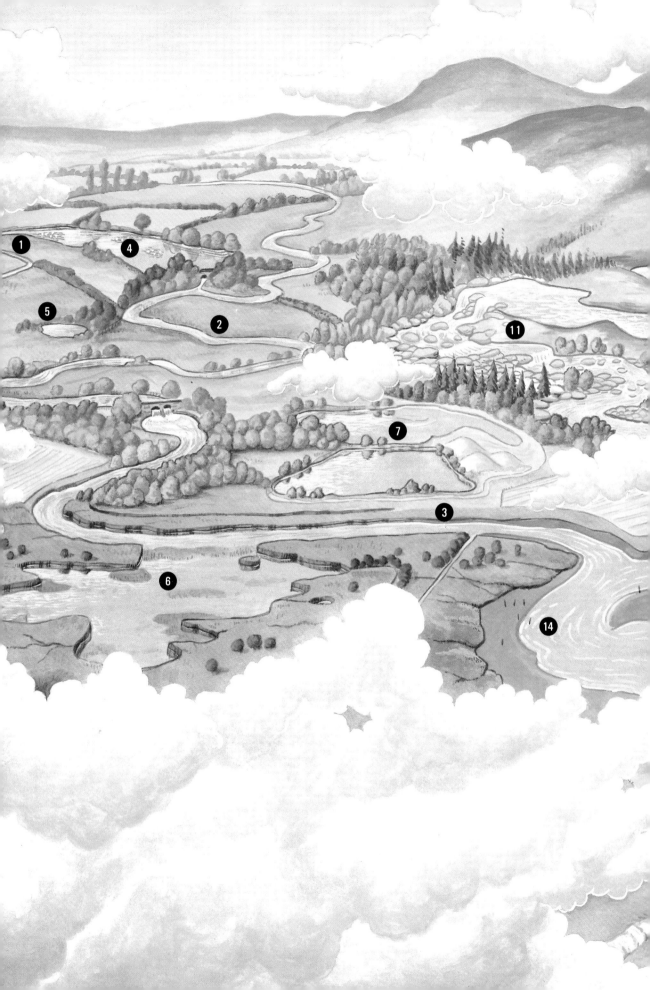

BARBEL

(Barbus barbus)

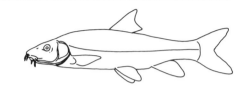

HABITAT

Although barbel occasionally occupy stretches of river where the pace is merely steady – even slow – if the choice exists they prefer well-oxygenated water with a strong flow over their heads and a well-scoured, clean sand or gravel bottom beneath them. Like chub, barbel love sanctuary swims, especially those with cover overhead, and this often results in these two species sharing a home: beneath undercut banks and submerged tree roots, or spots where rafts of cut weed and flotsam gather around trailing willow branches, thus diffusing the light; in fast runs between long, flowing beds of rununculus; at the tail end of weir-pools where the bottom shelves up and the flow increases; and in clean gravel runs between tall beds of bullrushes. Barbel also shoal up in 'open' deep runs despite a lack of weed and overhead cover as long as the water on the surface is broken and it is pushing through steadily close to the bottom.

DISTRIBUTION

Barbel are absent from Ireland and Scotland, and are present in Wales only in the River Wye, where they are slowly spreading after being introduced. Barbel have, in fact, been successfully stocked into several English river systems since the 1950s. They are still not exactly common, but rivers that enjoy large stocks are the Severn and its tributaries, the Thames and its tributaries, the Great Ouse, Hampshire Avon, Dorset Stour and several rivers in Yorkshire, which mark the barbel's northerly limit.

PHYSICAL CHARACTERISTICS

The barbel's unique elongated shape, large powerful fins and flat belly allow it to hold station close to the bottom in the strongest currents. Colouring is an olive brown along the back, gently fusing down the flanks into muted brass, with a creamy, off-white belly. The scales are small and deeply embedded, and lie very flat to the wiry body. Its fins are evenly coloured with a distinct warm tinge.

The pectorals are noticeably large and pointed. The top lobe of the deeply forked tail is pointed, the lower rounded.

The sloping, pointed snout with its underslung, semi-protrusible, vacuum-type mouth contains

FRANCE	**Farbeau**	SWEDEN	**Flodbarb**
GERMANY	**Barbe**	DENMARK	**Flodbarbe**
HOLLAND	**Barbeel**	SPAIN	**Barbo**
ITALY	**Barbo**		

WEIGHT RANGE

Average size:	**3-5 lb (1.35-2.25 kg)**
Specimen size:	**8-9 lb (3.6-4.1 kg)**
Record barbel:	**15 lb 7 oz (7.002 kg) caught by R. Morris, River Medway, Kent, 1993.**

four long, sensory barbels or whiskers. These immediately eliminate any confusion with and distinguish the barbel from its closest relatives, the loach (which sports six barbels) and the gudgeon (which has two).

REPRODUCTION

Barbel mass on the gravelly shallows to propagate their species, usually sometime in May. Like all cyprinids, the males sport tubercles on their noses and use these to nudge the swollen belly of the female in order to stimulate release of the eggs. A cloud of milt from a male quick enough to react (two, three or more males usually accompany each

female) fertilizes the small yellowy eggs as they tumble down through gaps in the gravel bed, where they hatch two weeks later.

FEEDING

Barbel use their long whiskers, which have super-sensitive taste pads at the tips, for probing down among weed and gravel for aquatic insect larvae, shrimps, crayfish and snails. They can create enormous suction with their protrusible mouth, hoovering up small fish such as minnows, loach and bullheads, and mincing them to a pulp with the pharyngeal teeth in the back of their throat.

Barbel feed most aggressively when there is a sudden increase in the river flow and in subdued light, especially during the hours of darkness.

FISHING FOR BARBEL

Barbel bite extremely boldly and are most easily caught by ledgering. Use large baits such as bread-crust, lobworms, cheesepaste and luncheon-meat cubes on a bomb or swan-shot link ledger. Small

baits such as sweetcorn, casters and maggots are best used in conjuction with a block-end feeder rig and quivertip indicator. Prebaiting the swim with stewed hempseed really attracts barbel and puts them into a feeding mood.

Finicky, clear-water barbel bite more freely from dusk onwards, even during mild winter evenings. In steady-paced marginal swims, stret peg with a float set well over depth, fixed to the line at both ends so it lies flat. Pinch on sufficient swan shot 12 in (30 cm) above the hook to anchor the

Its powerful, elongated shape, hoover-like mouth, large fins and four whiskers (or barbels) distinguish the barbel from other bottom feeders.

bait. Long, even-depth gravel runs can be trotted. Use a buoyant, squat float with all the shot fixed 12 in (30 cm) above the hook, and use breadcrust, maggots, worm, casters or sweetcorn while regularly introducing loose fragments of the same.

BLEAK

(Alburnus alburnus)

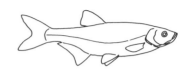

HABITAT
Bleak prefer sluggish rivers, where they live, often in huge shoals, feeding in the upper water layers close to the surface. They are also occasionally found in flooded gravel-pit complexes.

DISTRIBUTION
Bleak are absent from Ireland, Scotland and the west of Wales. Localised in England to certain river systems, such as the Thames and Great Ouse.

PHYSICAL CHARACTERISTICS
The bleak is an extremely thin, silvery and flat-sided cyprinid with a large eye and upturned, herring-like mouth. It has noticeably large scales, which are, in fact, used in the manufacture of imitation pearls. The fins are transparent light grey, sometimes yellowy or showing a touch of pink at the base. The tail is deeply forked and the anal fin is rather long, almost bream-like. Colouring changes from a blue-green sheen along the back to flanks of shimmering silver and a white belly.

REPRODUCTION
Spawning takes place during May or June, and the eggs are distributed over aquatic vegetation or stones.

FEEDING
During the warmer months, bleak feed actively close to the surface for midge and other aquatic insect larvae as they hatch, and for flies falling onto the surface. They dart about constantly, intercepting any free-falling items of food.

FISHING FOR BLEAK
Use small baits like a single maggot or caster presented 'on the drop' beneath a light float rig. Keep the shoal interested by regularly loosefeeding on the 'little and often' basis. Hook sizes 16 to 20 are ideal. Bleak are also fun to catch on a 9-12 ft (2.75-3.65 m) whip or short pole rigged with a line of the same length (to hand) for maximum efficiency.

Bleak are most effective livebaits for predators such as perch, chub and pike. Present one beneath a float using a single swan shot 12 in (30 cm) above the hook to keep the bait down. Use a large single

EUROPEAN NAMES

FRANCE	**Ablette**	HOLLAND	**Alver**
GERMANY	**Ukelei**	SWEDEN	**Loja**

WEIGHT RANGE

Average size: 3-5 in (7.5-12.5 cm)
Record bleak: 4¼ oz (120 kg) caught by B. Derrington, River Monnow, Wye mouth, Monmouthshire, 1982.

(size 4 is ideal) and hook the bait through both nostrils. Alternatively, present it as a deadbait. They can be wobbled on a 10 lb (4.5 kg) braided alasticum wire trace holding a duo of size 10 trebles, or offered completely static on the bottom for pike and zander. Alternatively, bleak may be ledgered on the bottom of fast runs for chub, or bumped across the current. Chub and especially big perch are really attracted to the bleak's silvery body, which is small and easy to swallow.

This delicate surface-feeder has flanks of burnished silver and a herring-like protruding bottom jaw.

15

BREAM

(Abramis brama)

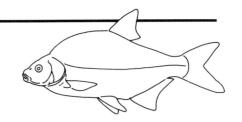

HABITAT

Bream prefer and abound in the largest shoals within the deepest areas of still and slow-moving coloured waters such as the Fenland Drains, the Norfolk Broads and interconnecting tidal rivers, the Irish lakes and most large river systems throughout England and southern Ireland. Clear-water reservoirs, lakes, gravel pits and meres breed the largest bream of all, especially where shoals are numerically low, allowing individual fish rich pickings with minimum competition.

Strangely, bream also fare well and reach large sizes in really fast, weedy and clear-flowing rivers. Weir-pools and confluence junctions are the hotspots.

DISTRIBUTION

Bream are unbelievably prolific throughout southern Ireland in most lakeland complexes and river systems, particularly the Erne and Shannon, but are found only in isolated lochs in southern Scotland. They are common throughout England, but localized in Wales.

PHYSICAL CHARACTERISTICS

The bream has a deep, compressed body with large fins and a fully protrusible mouth. Mature specimens have pronounced, hump backs. The small scales are covered in a tenacious, protective mucus to thwart irritation from parasites. Clear-water bream produce a noticeably much thinner layer of mucus. Colouring varies considerably between an overall silver in young bream, to the pale flanks and dark grey backs and fins of the adult fish. Mature, specimen bream from clear waters are more colourful, with dark brown backs fusing into flanks of golden bronze. The fins are a dark blue-grey and the extremely long anal fin may even show a touch of mauve. The tail is deeply forked.

During severe flooding, when canals and river systems run 'dirty', that distinct deep golden bronze of the bream completely disappears, leaving an overall pale, parchment-like colouring.

EUROPEAN NAMES			
FRANCE	**Brème**	ITALY	**Abramide**
GERMANY	**Brassen**	SWEDEN	**Braxen**
HOLLAND	**Brasm**	DENMARK	**Brasen**

WEIGHT RANGE	
Average size:	**2-3 lb (900 g-1.35 kg)**
Specimen size:	**8 lb plus (3.6 kg)**
Record bream:	**16 lb 9 oz (7.519 kg)**
	caught by M. McKeown,
	Southern Lake, 1991.

REPRODUCTION

Bream gather over the warm, weedy shallows in late spring, the aggressive males being easy to distinguish from the females by the knobbly, white spawning tubercles covering their heads and shoulders.

Spawning is often a noisy affair conducted in the upper water layers. It takes place throughout the night, even through to mid-morning, with up to several males servicing a single female, bumping into her swollen belly to ensure dispersal of the pale yellow eggs over soft weeds. The males simultaneously eject milt to fertilize the eggs, which hatch within 8-12 days.

FEEDING

Although bream do feed well off bottom, even intercepting descending food items during daylight hours, they feed most aggressively as a shoal unit from dusk onwards and throughout the night, browsing slowly over silty areas of the bottom and syphoning up desirable foods such as annelid worms and midge larvae (bloodworms) with their protrusible, hoover-like mouths. To do this they tilt their bodies and almost stand on their heads. Large shoals of adult bream can consume vast amounts of food, hence the need for heavy groundbaiting to attract and keep them in a given area.

FISHING FOR BREAM

Bream do not like chasing their food, so endeavour to offer the bait just off or lying completely static on the bottom. In slow-moving rivers and when fishing at short range in stillwaters, present baits like sweetcorn, stewed wheat, maggots, casters, breadflake or worms using a simple waggler or lift rig. In wide rivers, ledger using an open-end, breadcrumb-packed feeder, fixed paternoster rig and quivertip indicator to register sensitive forward and drop-back bites.

When fishing large stillwaters, a bobbin or monkey-climber indicator/electric bite-alarm combination is imperative for distant swims. Big baits like breadflake or a lobworm on a size 8-6 hook invariably prove selective and result in larger-than-average bream.

Even large bream can be landed with a long pole, which offers superior presentation of float tackle in both still and running water in depths of 15 ft (4.5 m) plus, where all standard float techniques except the slider are impractical.

The common bream is unmistakable: dark grey fins, a deeply forked tail, and deep, golden bronze flanks covered in a thick protective layer of mucus.

BREAM/RUDD HYBRID

Thick-set, muted golden bronze flanks, scales noticeably larger than a true bream, red-brown fins and lips that are usually level; without doubt this is a bream/rudd hybrid.

While this particular hybrid is extremely common in southern Ireland, it is comparatively rare elsewhere within the British Isles.

DISTINGUISHING FEATURES

Bream/rudd are thick-set, powerful fighters reaching weights in excess of 5 lb (2.25 kg) and averaging 2-4 lb (900 g-1.8 kg) when adult. They retain the bream's depth of body, with slightly larger, rudd-like scales, and noticeably muted golden-bronze flanks with red-brown fins. There is no mistaking this hybrid's parentage for anything else but bream and rudd, and they are highly prized by most visiting coarse fishermen in the Republic of Ireland. Many visitors do in fact prefer catching these colourful hybrids to breams.

19

SILVER BREAM

(Blicca bjoerkna)

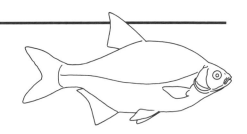

HABITAT
The silver bream likes slow-moving rivers, canals, irrigation channels and lakes.

DISTRIBUTION
Although once quite common, it is a rare species nowadays with isolated populations confined to East Anglia and the Midlands. It is absent from Ireland and Scotland.

PHYSICAL CHARACTERISTICS
As few fishermen ever get to see a true silver bream, let alone catch one, it is not an easy species to identify or to distinguish from roach/bream hybrids. The silver bream is a delicate-looking fish, and is not covered in a heavy layer of mucus like the common bream. It has a small head and noticeably large eye. The scales are quite large and distinctly 'silvery'. Enthusiasts who keep tropical freshwater fish will certainly draw a comparison between silver bream and the tinfoil barb. When erect, the silver bream's dorsal fin is unusually high, and its pectoral, pelvic and anal fins usually show a pinkish tinge, rather like a dace.

Unfortunately, some of these characteristics are also shared by roach/bream hybrids, so identification is rather difficult, especially taking into account this fish's relative rarity.

REPRODUCTION
Silver bream spawn in the late spring and will hybridize with common bream, roach or rudd.

FEEDING
It actively feeds between mid-water and the bottom, preferring a staple diet of aquatic insect larvae, snails, shrimps, daphnia, and so on.

FISHING FOR SILVER BREAM
There is no method guaranteed to catch, or that is particularly suitable to lure silver bream. All light floatfishing techniques used for rudd, roach and bream will tempt silver bream if they are present.

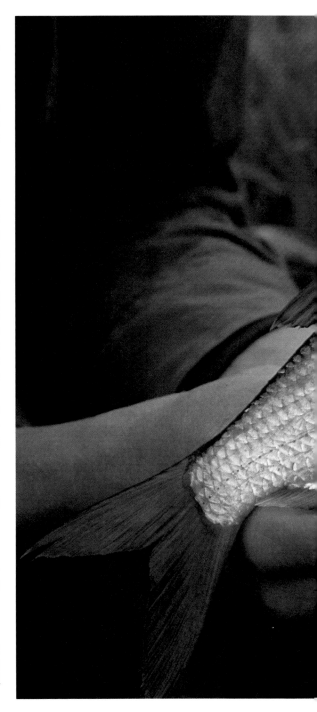

EUROPEAN NAMES

FRANCE	**Brême**	ITALY	**Abramide**
	Bordelière	SWEDEN	**Björkna**
GERMANY	**Güster**	DENMARK	**Flive**
HOLLAND	**Kolblei**		

WEIGHT RANGE

Average size:	**6 oz (170 g)**
Specimen size:	**10 oz (285 g)**
Record silver bream:	**15 oz (425 g) caught by D. Flack, Grime Spring, Lakenheath, Suffolk, 1988.**

A clean, virtually slimeless, delicate body, large eye and pinky warm fins are the features distinguishing the silver from the common bream.

BULLHEAD

(Cottus gobio)

HABITAT
The bullhead spends the greater part of its existence on the river bottom, beneath the protection of rocks and large stones, where it quickly darts from one to another to avoid being eaten. It prefers swift, clean-flowing rivers and streams, but will tolerate sluggish ditches.

DISTRIBUTION
The species is common throughout England and Wales, but is not found in Ireland or Scotland.

PHYSICAL CHARACTERISTICS
The bullhead has a wide, flattish head (hence its nickname 'Miller's Thumb') with a cavernous mouth, noticeably large pectoral fins, and a rapidly tapering body with a distinctly rounded tail. It has two dorsal fins; the first has spines, the second soft rays only. There are more spines on the edge of the gill cover. It has a tough, scale-less, light grey body, heavily marked with irregular dark brown blotches. The fins are also flecked with dark brown markings, and the belly is off-white. It often lies on the bottom with its body in a curled position.

REPRODUCTION
The bullhead spawns in the spring, depositing a clump of sticky eggs on the underside of a rock or large stone or in a carefully prepared depression. These are guarded by the male until the fry emerge around 20 days later.

FEEDING
It is an aggressive predator of other fish's eggs and fry, and also feeds on freshwater shrimps and aquatic insect larvae.

FISHING FOR BULLHEAD
Only schoolboys specifically set out to catch bullheads, which readily gobble up pieces of worm fished beside rocks on the bottom of sluggish streams. However, they are much relished by other predators, and make fine live or dead baits for

Bulbous, flattened head, cavernous mouth, mottled brown and light grey body, large pectoral fins and piggy eyes; these features belong only to the bullhead.

chub and trout. Present one on a size 4 hook beneath a chunky Avon-type float or simply free-line it through deep runs beneath overhangs. You can quickly collect a supply of bullheads for bait by holding an aquarium-type (square) net tight against the bottom immediately downstream of any large stone and using the current strength to whisk them into it as you raise the stone.

EUROPEAN NAMES

FRANCE	**Chabot**	HOLLAND	**Rivier-**
GERMANY	**Groppe**		**donderpad**
		SWEDEN	**Stensimpa**

WEIGHT RANGE

Average size: **2-4 in (5-10 cm)**

Record bullhead: **1 oz (28 g) caught by R. Johnson, Bramley & Shamley Green River, Surrey, 1983.**

CRUCIAN CARP

(Carassius carassius)

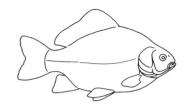

HABITAT

This gentle, rounded fish is a lover of stillwaters, and rarely fares well in rivers. Although crucian carp do thrive in coloured ponds and lakes that are completely devoid of vegetation, wherever they have the choice they will never be far from reed-lines or lilies. They generally shoal according to their year class, which results in large catches of small, hand-sized crucians or limited numbers of very much larger specimens of 1 lb (450 g) up-wards. In exceptionally rich, clear lakes and pits prolific in both marginal and surface vegetation, but low in competition species, it is possible to catch good-quality crucian carp in quantity.

DISTRIBUTION

Crucian carp are common throughout England, particularly in East Anglia, in small ponds, pits and lakes, but not found in Ireland or Scotland.

This gentle, fully-scaled carp has deep, evenly coloured flanks of buttery bronze, and an upturned mouth. Chris Turnbull knows how to catch *and* paint them.

EUROPEAN NAMES			
FRANCE	**Carassin**	ITALY	**Carassio**
GERMANY	**See Karausche**	SWEDEN	**Ruda**
		DENMARK	**Karuss**
HOLLAND	**Kroes-karper**	SPAIN	**Carpin**

WEIGHT RANGE

Average size:	**8 oz-1¼ lb (225-560 g)**
Specimen size:	**over 2 lb (900 g)**
Record crucian carp:	**5 lb 10½ oz (2.565 kg) caught by G. Halls, lake near King's Lynn, Norfolk, 1976.**

PHYSICAL CHARACTERISTICS

Size for size, the crucian has the deepest, most compressed, hump-backed body of all carps. It has a distinct and even scale pattern, and is beautifully coloured in an overall buttery bronze. Its fins are an even, warm, grey-brown hue, and are all nicely rounded, including the long dorsal fin, whereas the first dorsal ray of other carps, even the goldfish, is decidedly upright. By this fact alone it is easy to identify the crucian, which also has a small, neat, slightly upturned mouth and no barbels.

REPRODUCTION

Crucian carp gather in the warm shallows in late spring – sometimes as late as June – where they distribute their tiny, yellowy eggs over sunken marginal grasses, rushes and reedlines, or over beds of soft, rooted weeds.

FEEDING

Crucians are among the most deliberate of all bot-tom-feeding fish, consuming all forms of aquatic insect larvae, such as bloodworms, snails and shrimps. They also eat an amount of algae and soft plant tissue. The clusters of up to a dozen dis-tinctive, tiny feeding bubbles that rise to the

surface when crucians are standing on their heads and rooting along the bottom, make the species easy to locate during the summer months. They also give away their position by cavorting high up out of the water every so often, in all probability to clear their gills from bottom silt and debris – just like the larger carps.

FISHING FOR CRUCIANS

Because they often stand on their heads to suck in the bait from the bottom, just like tench, float-fishing with the lift method – with a small shot pinched on the line just 2 in (5 cm) from the hook – is the most effective way of catching crucian carp. Very often registration, even on a delicately shotted float, barely produces a strikable bite, so floatfishing is always preferable to ledgering. Use hooks in sizes 18 to 10 and baits such as maggots, sweetcorn, brandlings, breakflake and breadcrust in conjunction with loose feed or small balls of cereal groundbait. With the bait presented just on or just off bottom, hit any dip or lift of the float, no matter how slight. Fishing after dark in clear-water fisheries will produce the reluctant specimens.

CRUCIAN CARP HYBRIDS

In small, densely stocked ponds and pits, hybridization regularly occurs with other carp gathered in the spawning area at the same time, and particularly with the fully-scaled king common or wild carp, goldfish and even multi-coloured varieties like shubunkins.

The parentage of many of these crosses is not easy to distinguish. If you are unsure about the authenticity of a particular wild or crucian carp, look at the barbels. Common or wild carp/crucian hybrids, for instance, have considerably smaller barbels than the true carp would possess for its size. And whatever its size, a true crucian does not have any barbels, nor the slightest hint of a protrusible, underslung mouth.

If a carp possesses the characteristics of both the crucian and the common or wild carp, as this fish does, immediately suspect a hybrid, which invariably has tiny barbels.

GRASS CARP

(Ctenopharyngodon idella)

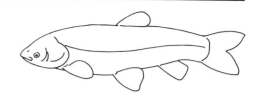

HABITAT

This Asian import likes both still and slow-moving water, preferably containing a lush environment full of aquatic plants, especially soft weeds. It can nevertheless fare well on algae growth, even in small, coloured, man-made pits and ponds where rooted plants are completely absent. It was originally imported by river authorities and aquarists to reduce and control soft weed growth.

DISTRIBUTION

The grass carp is limited to isolated pits, ponds, lakes and irrigation channels in England and Wales, particularly in East Anglia and Kent where it has been deliberately introduced as an angler's fish. It is absent from Scotland and Ireland.

EUROPEAN NAMES	
GERMANY	**Graeskarpe**

WEIGHT RANGE	
Average size:	**3-6 lb (1.35-2.7 kg)**
Specimen size:	**Over 10 lb (4.5 kg)**
Record grass carp:	**23 lb 14 oz (10.839 kg) caught by G. Wallis, Moneycroft Fisheries, Kent, 1991.**

PHYSICAL CHARACTERISTICS

At first glance the grass carp looks very similar to the chub due to its torpedo shape and even, fully-

scaled body. It is even similarly coloured with a dark grey to brown back, brassy-pewter flanks and creamy white belly. Its tail, however, is noticeably larger and more deeply forked. The dorsal fin starts further forward than that of the chub, well ahead of a vertical line drawn from the leading edge of the pelvic fin. Its most noticeable, distinguishing features, however, are the extremely low-set eyes, which are level with the corner of its relatively neat mouth. Chub of the same size possess larger mouths. Moreover, grass carp have the potential to reach weights in excess of 30 lb (13.5 kg) in temperate countries, and have been recorded in excess of twice this size in Asia.

REPRODUCTION

The grass carp is indigenous to the Amur river system of China, and it is generally accepted that it cannot reproduce in the wild in British fresh water because in Asia the eggs, which are laid in the spring, need to drift with warm currents in temperatures above 65°F (18°C) for many miles prior to hatching.

FEEDING

It is an enthusiastic top-water feeder, and often hovers nearly stationary just beneath the surface, with its head angled slightly upwards. It is very deliberate in its feeding habits, consuming soft plant tissue in large quantities when water temperatures exceed 70°F (21°C). It also picks up food, including the baits of carp fishermen – such as peanuts, sweetcorn, bread and pastes – from the bottom.

FISHING FOR GRASS CARP

Grass carp can be caught by either ledgering or presenting the lift method on bottom-fished baits. However, they are more easily taken on baits – breadcrust, trout pellets, floating boilies – offered in the surface film, in conjunction with a floating controller such as the 'tenpin', stopped 3 ft (90 cm) from the hook with a small bead and stop knot. Use hook sizes 12-8.

They also respond to baits suspended at mid water and those that slowly descend from the surface. Standard carp tackle and a line test of 6-12 lb (2.7-5.45 kg) are ideal.

The grass carp's strange, low-set eye and small, mullet-like mouth are the features which immediately distinguish it from the chub.

KING CARP

(Cyprinus carpio)

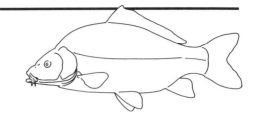

HABITAT

King carp will live virtually anywhere except in cold, fast, rocky, spate rivers. They prefer ponds, pits and lakes, growing to their largest proportions in those containing prolific plant growth and a rich larder of natural food. They also fare well in slow-moving, lowland rivers and canals.

DISTRIBUTION

Owing to their quick growth and durability, king carp have become the most widely stocked of all freshwater fish within the British Isles – not only in stillwaters, but throughout many river systems as well. Only in Ireland and Scotland are they still comparatively thin on the ground.

PHYSICAL CHARACTERISTICS

King carp have all the wild carp's good qualities, plus – owing to selective breeding by European fish farmers over the past century – a much-increased growth rate and a massive ultimate weight potential. Although their shapes vary enormously, king carp varieties are much thicker in cross-section than the wild strain, with increased depth in the region of the shoulders. Moreover, king carp vary enormously in their scaleage, from fully-scaled 'commons' to the completely scale-less leather carp.

Between these two extremes, those with scales running only along the lateral line are called linears. Those with irregularly shaped scales covering the entire body are called fully-scaled mirror carp. Those with odd clusters of really large scales are referred to as plated mirror carp. Starbursts have countless small scales scattered all over their flanks and bellies. Standard mirror carp have a plain, irregular scaleage with just the odd group of scales, usually along the back and in the tail region. The permutations are endless and help to make the king carp such an interesting, exciting and beautiful adversary.

Colouring also varies considerably, from blue-grey or bronze, to sandy-beige along the back, to

EUROPEAN NAMES

FRANCE	**Carpe**	SWEDEN	**Karp**
GERMANY	**Karpfen**	DENMARK	**Karpe**
HOLLAND	**Karper**	SPAIN	**Carpa**
ITALY	**Carpa**		

WEIGHT RANGE

Average size:	5-12 lb (2.25-5.45 kg)
Specimen size:	Over 20-25 lb (9-11.35 kg)
Record king carp:	51 lb 8 oz (23.358 kg) caught by C. Yates, Redmire Pool, 1980.

King carp are noticeably deeper than wild carp, with tremendous variation in scaleage, from the fully-scaled 'common' (top), to the completely scaleless 'leather' (bottom).

Chris Turnbull Oct 93

sides of pale grey, yellow, beige, pewter or golden bronze. The fins can be all grey, but generally show a tinge of warmth in the anal and lower half of the tail. Just like the fish that started carp culture, the original wild carp, king carp have four long, sensory barbels, two at the corner of each jaw hinge. Each barbel has a taste pad on the extreme tip.

REPRODUCTION

King carp spawn during the same late spring-early summer (May to June) period as wild carp, using any available medium on which to lay their pale, translucent eggs – reed stems, willow or alder roots, or among soft weeds. The fry hatch after 6-10 days and feed on microscopic plankton. In fisheries containing a varied stock of 'mixed carps', interbreeding occurs regularly. Wildies spawn with king carp, mirrors with leathers, crucians with king or wild carp, creating both hybrids and stunningly beautiful king carp variants (see Crucian carp and Coloured king carp variants). In small ponds,pits and lakes where the water is thick in green planktons or contains a dense jungle of aquatic plants, particularly soft, rooted weeds like Canadian pondweed and hornwort, fry survival is considerably higher than in clearwater fisheries sparse in vegetation.

Arguably the most attractive of all king carp scale patterns is the 'plated mirror'.

FEEDING

Sizeable king carp are the most dominant and glut-
tonous of all freshwater fish when feeding in
earnest. They can create deep, circular holes in the
bottom of silty lakes while rooting for bloodworms, crunch through the shell of a mussel with
their powerful throat (pharyngeal) teeth, and consume vast quantities of both their own eggs and fry
and those of other species. Their staple diet consists of aquatic insect larvae and crustacea, and the
large 'feeding bubbles' that spew to the surface
when king carp are heavily engrossed in bottom-
feeding help the fisherman enormously in locating
them; as does the wonderful sight of them slurping
down floating baits from the surface.

FISHING FOR KING CARP

King carp respond to simple floatfishing techniques, especially the lift method, just like the
'wildie'. In heavily fished waters, a cube of luncheon meat, boilie or peanut rigged on a short hair

Almost a 'fully scaled mirror' above, and below, a 'linear
mirror' with a row of scales along the lateral line.

encourages more confident bites. Large baits such
as chunks of paste, worms or mussels can be freelined, and the line watched for indications of the
carp moving off.

Use the shock (or bolt) rig with the bait on a fine
hair in conjuction with a 1½-3 oz (85 g) fixed or
semi-fixed bomb for educated carp, so they 'bolt'
off and set the hook themselves, as opposed to
spitting out the bait. Use strong hooks in sizes 8-4.
You can freeline surface baits or present them with
a floating controller to gain extra distance. Gear
tackle strength to the situation in hand and size of
carp you expect. A 6-8 lb (2.7-3.6 kg) outfit is ideal
for snag-free waters, while a step up to lines of
10-14 lb (4.5-6.35 kg) is imperative when trying to
extract carp from overgrown, snaggy spots, or to
subdue monsters. Using underpowered tackle for
really big carp is only asking for trouble.

'COLOURED' KING CARP VARIANTS (METALLIC CARP)

Everything mentioned about the wild carp and its cultivated king carp counterpart also applies to coloured carp because all are sports or strains from the original, natural, fully-scaled Chinese carp. An orange or pure white koi carp in someone's garden pond, for instance, may seem an entirely different species from carp in the local gravel pit, but they share the same Latin name and are, from a genetic point of view, the same creature.

This is why they are able to inter-breed freely and throw up so many interesting variants, not only in scaleage, but also in colour. Isolated fisheries are now stocking these king carp, coloured crosses in addition to natural carp, and the permutations are endless.

Some of the most attractive and commonly bred variants are called 'metallic' carp due to the metallic look of their koi carp parentage. In colour, these carp vary between muted shades of burnished beige, gold, silver and pewter, and have distinct etching across the head – hence their nickname, 'ghost koi', because in coloured water very often all that can be seen are the skull markings.

Right: Variants like this golden-beige 'plated mirror' and the common scaled hi-goi are the result of cross-breeding king carp with koi. These fish fight hard and are fun to catch.
Below: Cross-breeding the common scaled king carp with a white or silver koi carp produces these 'ghost koi' or 'metallics' in various tones of pewter, silver, gold or beige.

WILD CARP

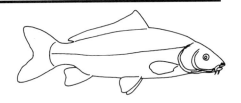

(Cyprinus carpio)

HABITAT

The wild carp fares best in shallow, warm water, coloured ponds and lakes whether the bottom is hard or silty.

DISTRIBUTION

Owing to the widespread introduction of the fast-growing and heavier king carp strains (see King carp and variants) throughout much of the British Isles during the 20th century, only a few isolated fisheries can still boast a stock of truly wild carp, or 'wildies'.

PHYSICAL CHARACTERISTICS

Wild carp originated in Asia and were introduced into British waters by German monks during the Middle Ages as food to harvest from their monastery stew-ponds. Although they are classified with king carp as *Cyprinus carpio*, indicating that there is no genetic difference between wild carp and the cultivated, distinctly 'hump-backed' king carp strains, 'wildies' are naturally slimmer, slower growing, and rarely top 10 lb (4.5 kg) in British waters.

Wild carp are long, barbel shaped and fully scaled, with the regulation four long whiskers or barbels, two set on each corner of the semi-protrusible, hoover-like mouth.

The fins are pale grey and large, especially the paddle-like tail, which often shows a touch of pale orange, as does the anal fin. Body colouring varies according to the water colour. In sandy or 'pea green' water, for instance, the back is sandy-brown fusing into flanks of pale bronze. Yet in clear water a stunning golden bronze covers the entire carp. Only in fisheries where every single carp is distinctly barbel shaped, fully scaled, lean and with big fins, and all look like peas from the same pod, are those fish likely to be true 'wildies'.

REPRODUCTION

Wild carp spawn during May or June, the females carpeting marginal plant stems and soft weeds with their eggs, which are simultaneously fertilized with milt from the males. The crashing noise made

Chris Turnbull '93.

EUROPEAN NAMES			
FRANCE	Carpe	SWEDEN	Karp
GERMANY	Karpfen	DENMARK	Karpe
HOLLAND	Karper	SPAIN	Carpe
ITALY	Carpa		

WEIGHT RANGE	
Average size:	2-3 lb (900 g-1.35 kg)
Specimen size:	Over 8 lb (3.6 kg)
Record wild carp:	No separate classification, see King carp.

by spawning carp can be heard, and the commotion seen, from up to 100 yds (91 m) away. In coloured water a high percentage of fry survives, resulting in very over-stocked ponds full of ever-hungry, slim, wiry, wild carp.

FEEDING

Wild carp root along the bottom in search of food such as shrimps, midge larvae, annelid worms, which they hoover up along with copious amounts of detritus. Long lines of 'feeding' bubbles spew up to the surface during aggressive feeding spells, which usually occur at dawn and sometimes at dusk. The colour of the water can be observed, and the exact location of the fish pinpointed, when several 'wildies' are feeding in earnest.

FISHING FOR 'WILDIES'

They are fun to catch at close range on float tackle, using an 11-12 ft (3.35-3.65 m) match/float rod coupled to a 4 lb (1.8 kg) test reel line and hooks in sizes 12-8. Present a waggler float lift style, using maggots, redworms, sweetcorn, breadflake or paste. Alternatively, ledger a cube of luncheon meat, a huge lobworm, or the large, orange insides of a swan mussel on a size 6 hook tied direct to 6 lb (2.7 kg) test used with an Avon-style rod combo. Fish light to enjoy fully this carp's sporting qualities.

Long, slim, fully scaled and hard-fighting; only in fisheries where every single carp looks exactly the same are you likely to find true wild carp.

CHARR

(Salvelinus alpinus)

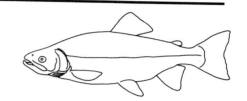

HABITAT

A shoaling fish of the Salmonidae family, the charr prefers the deep, cold, pure water of lakes and lochs, where it resides usually at great depths, except during its reproductive cycle, when it may enter rivers and streams.

DISTRIBUTION

It is found in Ireland, Wales, the Lake District and in Scotland.

PHYSICAL CHARACTERISTICS

There are numerous strains of British charr, most of which have been landlocked for thousands of years, and subsequently formed their own identity and very definite mosaic-like colour patterns. The charr is slow-growing, and trout-like in shape, with a small, neat head, large eye and small scales. It is usually greeny-blue or pewter along the back, fusing into lower flanks and a belly of pale orange, scattered with white and orange spots. Colouring

intensifies during the spawning cycle, particularly with male fish, which sport vivid orange-red bellies. There is absolutely no way of confusing the charr with other speices. The pectoral, pelvic and anal fins have a warm, 'pinky' hue, and their leading edges have a distinct white line. The tail is noticeably forked, not square.

REPRODUCTION

Within the Arctic region this very same species is called the Arctic charr, and it migrates from the sea into fresh water to spawn just like salmon and seatrout. Those existing in British stillwaters lay their eggs sometime between December and April over the rocky lake bottom, or enter mountain rivers or streams, where the hen fish excavates a redd (depression) in the gravel bottom. The eggs take several weeks to hatch.

FEEDING

While charr feed heavily on plankton, they also consume a typical trout diet of aquatic insect larvae, crustacea, molluscs and small shoal fish like the whitefishes, and the parr of all trout, including their own kind.

FISHING FOR CHARR

Charr are most easily tracked down prior to the spawning season, when they leave the deeps and

Left: This jumbo-sized charr caught from a Scottish river on a tiny spinner, typifies the species colouring. Note the distinct white edges to the lower fins.

Above: A trout in both shape and characteristics, the charr is easily identified by its unique orange-to-red belly, which intensifies during the spawning season.

gather in river entrances. Light spinning tackle, using a 6 lb (2.7 kg) test line and size 1-3 mepps, small spoons or a small toby-like lure, is ideal. Charr are often caught on flies intended for brown trout. Charr fishermen in the Lake District troll slowly with heavy downrigger leads, to which they attach a series of small lures, in order to search at great depths – sometimes down to as much as 100 ft (30 m).

The secret to success with the enigmatic charr is anticipating exactly where and when they are most likely to gather en masse, prior to their eventually spawning.

Local knowledge is invaluable and the nearest tackle shop is the best source of information.

EUROPEAN NAMES

FRANCE	**L'Omble Chevalier**	SWEDEN	**Röding**
		DENMARK	**Fjeldørred**
GERMANY	**Seesaibling**	SPAIN	**La Truita**
HOLLAND	**Schotje**		**de Rierol**
ITALY	**Salmorino di Montagna**		

WEIGHT RANGE

Average size:	**8 oz-1¼ lb (225-560 g)**
Specimen size:	**Over 2 lb (900 g)**
Record charr:	**7 lb 7 oz (3.373 kg) caught by J. Macdonald, Loch Arkaig, Fort William, Inverness-shire, 1990.**

CHANNEL CATFISH

(Ictalurus punctatus)

HABITAT

The channel catfish is most prolific in deep, coloured rivers with a good flow (it loves weir- and dam-pools) in North America, from where it originates. It also lives happily in European modern, man-made, coloured fisheries – old clay, sand and gravel pits – and even in shallow, densely stocked fisheries with the biomass angled towards carp.

DISTRIBUTION

Although originally imported into the UK for the aquarium and ornamental pond-fish trade, the channel catfish has found its way into a limited number of stillwater fisheries throughout southern England, and will, no doubt, provide exciting sport in the future.

PHYSICAL CHARACTERISTICS

It has a long and thick-set, powerful, scale-less body with a wide, flattish head. Its mouth is equally wide, with bristle-like pads of fine 'holding' teeth just inside both the upper and lower jaws. There is a long barbel extending from each corner of the upper lip, which noticeably protrudes. There are two small, erect barbels on top of the snout, and four similar ones under the chin, making eight whiskers in all. The overall colouring along the back and flanks is pale to dark grey, and the belly is white. It has a short, erect dorsal fin, a large rubbery adipose fin, a long anal fin and a deeply forked tail. All fins are an even, dark grey. The eyes are small and 'piggy'.

REPRODUCTION

The species spawns in late spring or early summer, and likes to migrate into streams or small rivers.

FEEDING

Largely a bottom scavenger, eating worms, molluscs and small shoal fish, channel catfish do sometimes hunt in the upper water layers, particularly during high water temperatures. It slams the water with its tail when it surfaces.

Sporting no less than eight whiskers (two of which are long ones) from a wide, cavernous mouth, the channel catfish has a grey body, deeply forked tail, adipose fin and short erect dorsal fin.

FISHING FOR CHANNEL CATS

You are most likely to catch one while seeking other bottom-feeding species. It will even gobble up baits such as corn, bread and maggots, but much prefers worms, mussels, cockles, small freshly-killed fish or a fresh cutlet from a larger fish. It is usually a most aggressive feeder throughout the summer, even during bright sunshine, but is known for dropping the bait if it feels undue resistance. There is no need to fish for it after dark. Freeline or ledger the bait on standard carp tackle, using hook sizes 4-1/0. Allow a few feet of line to be taken without resistance before striking.

EUROPEAN NAMES

NONE

WEIGHT RANGE

Average size:	3-6 lb (1.35-2.7 kg)
Specimen size:	10 lb plus (4.5 kg)
Record channel catfish:	None at present. Not uncommon over 30 lb (13.6 kg) in North America, where the record stands in excess of 50 lb (22.7 kg).

WELS CATFISH

(Silurus glanis)

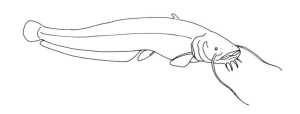

HABITAT

Being largely nocturnal and a bottom feeder, the wels loves the sanctuary of deep, dark gullies and hideouts such as undercut banks, sunken trees and dense, overhanging marginal vegetation where it can rest during daylight. It fares well in fisheries where the water is heavily coloured – even ones lacking any natural or man-made structures or features. It especially likes waters containing good stocks of fodder species such as small roach, rudd, bream and crucian carp, and those where the bottom is muddy or heavily silted.

DISTRIBUTION

It is generally confined to English stillwater lakes, reservoirs and gravel pits where it has been deliberately introduced, although it is common in many river systems throughout Europe. It is absent from Wales, Scotland and Ireland.

PHYSICAL CHARACTERISTICS

The wels is arguably one of the largest, if not *the* largest freshwater fish in the world. It has been taken in Russia by commercial fishermen to over 400 lb (180 kg). It has a smooth, long, scale-less, tapering body, not unlike a giant tadpole, with around two-thirds of its bodyweight concentrated in the first third of its length. The huge head is broad and flattened with a wide mouth, in which it holds its prey with the bristle-like pads of fine teeth that line the jaws. The eyes are tiny and situated on top of the head, and in front of them are two long feelers or barbels used as ultra-sensitive feeding probes. Should the prey touch one of these barbels when they are angled forwards, it is immediately vacuumed back into the cavernous mouth. Sprouting from under its chin are four short sensory barbels, making a total of six in all.

Colouring is usually a dark grey-brown along the back, fusing downwards along the flanks into a mosaic of mottled olive, brown and mauve. The belly is light grey. The wels has a small, erect dorsal fin, large pectorals, small pelvics and then a long, continuous anal fin, which almost blends into the small, squared-off tail. It is most unlikely to be mistaken for any other species.

REPRODUCTION

The wels spawns during June or July, the female depositing her eggs in a large clump or mass into a nest prepared by the male. This nest is usually a depression in the bottom, and is sometimes lined with remnants of marginal growth. Once fertilization has taken place, the eggs are guarded by the male throughout the incubation period.

FEEDING

The wels is a voracious feeder, particularly in low light values. There is little that finds its way into fresh water that an adult wels will not attempt to eat. Fish of up to half its own size are considered fair game, along with waterfowl, frogs, toads, newts and rodents such as voles and rats. It generally scavenges along the bottom, but will on occasion feed from the surface.

FISHING FOR CATFISH

The wels should be considered a summer species, as this is when it is most active. It readily hoovers up ledgered, smelly paste baits, mussels, worms, livebaits, deadbaits, squid, liver, large fish-based boilies and so use size 2-2/0 hooks tied direct to a 12-15 lb (5.45-6.8 kg) reel line. Where big fish are expected, use a 2 ft (60 cm) mono trace of 20-30 lb (9-13.6 kg) test. Simply freeline the bait if fishing at close range, up to about 10-15 yd (m). The best results occur from dusk until dawn, although in heavily coloured, green-water fisheries, expect runs at any time of the day, especially during periods of high water temperatures and during humid, thundery or overcast conditions.

Overleaf: The wels catfish has a smooth, tadpole-like body of mottled olive green, mauve and brown, a huge head, two extremely long whiskers (six in all), a tiny dorsal (no adipose) and a squared tail almost jointed to the anal fin.

EUROPEAN NAMES

FRANCE	**Siluro**	SWEDEN	**Mal**
GERMANY	**Wels**	DENMARK	**Malle**
HOLLAND	**Meerval**	SPAIN	**Siluro**
ITALY	**Siluro**		

WEIGHT RANGE

Average size:	**5-15 lbs (2.25-6.8 kg)**
Specimen size:	**Over 25 lb (11.35 kg)**
Record catfish:	**43 lb 8 oz (19.730 kg) caught by R. J. Bray, Wilstone Reservoir, Tring, Hertfordshire, 1970.**

CHUB

(Leuciscus cephalus)

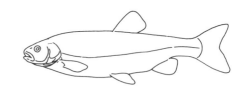

HABITAT

Wherever they have the choice, chub prefer a roof over their heads, or at least one close by, beneath which they can retreat in times of danger. Features such as the dense canopy provided by overhanging trees, weedrafts, bridges, long flowering beds of streamer weed and undercut banks attract chub like bees to a honeypot.

Chub love fast, well-oxygenated water, weir-pools especially, but are perhaps most prolific in medium-paced rivers, particularly where trees, bushes and reed or rush beds provide cover along the margins. They shoal up in good numbers in sluggish, coloured rivers like the Great Ouse and Thames, and even fare well in stillwaters, particularly in gravel pits.

DISTRIBUTION

Excluding Devon and Cornwall, chub are common in most river systems throughout England, but are rare in Wales except in the River Wye and its tributaries, which breeds a prolific stock. They are present only in the southern-most of Scottish rivers, and are completely absent from Ireland.

PHYSICAL CHARACTERISTICS

Its decidedly torpedo-shaped body, blunt, cigar-like head and large mouth with thick-rimmed lips make the chub easily distinguishable from dace and roach, which have much smaller mouths. In addition, both the dorsal and anal fins of the chub are rounded, or convex, compared to those of the dace and roach, which curve inwards.

Colouring is dark grey to brown along the back, fusing into brassy flanks and a creamy white belly. The largish scales are noticeably less brassy during the winter months – more pewter-like. The dorsal fin and slightly pointed tail are dark grey, the pectoral is translucent grey, and the pelvic and anal fins have a pale orange tint.

REPRODUCTION

Chub gather to spawn in the fastest, most gravelly shallow water during May, although this could occur a month later or even a month earlier, depending upon water conditions. The act of spawning is an incredibly noisy affair as each female, often accompanied by more than one male, crashes and shudders through mere inches of water, distributing a stream of eggs over willow moss or the gravel bottom. Like all cyprinids, the males, which are distinguished by the small, white tubercles covering their heads and shoulders, simultaneously emit a spray of milt over the eggs to ensure fertilization.

The fry hatch within 10 days and consume minute plankton until they are about 2 in (5 cm) long, when they can manage aquatic insect larvae, and later on small fishes, etc.

FEEDING

Chub are an aggressive shoal fish and arguably the greediest of all the UK's freshwater species. While they will slurp in a huge chunk of breadcrust off the surface during the summer months, they can also be frustratingly deliberate about sucking in a single caster or maggot once winter sets in and the water turns gin clear. Chub consume all forms of aquatic insect life, plus crustacea, newts, frogs and toads. Fitted with a powerful pair of pharyngeal teeth in its throat, a chub also happily minces up small fish like minnows and bleak, while an adult chub of 4 lb (1.8 kg) will think nothing of engulfing a 6 in (15 cm) roach. Chub do in fact consume smaller fishes as a substantial part of their diet, far more so than most anglers realize.

EUROPEAN NAMES

FRANCE	Chevesne	SWEDEN	Färna
GERMANY	Döbel	DENMARK	Døbel
HOLLAND	Meun	SPAIN	Cacho
ITALY	Cavedano		

WEIGHT RANGE

Average size: **1½–3 lb (680 g-1.35 kg)**
Specimen size: **5 lb (2.25 g)**
Record chub: **8 lb 4 oz (3.743 kg)**
caught by G. F. Smith,
River Avon, Christchurch,
1913.

Chris Turnbull 98

FISHING FOR CHUB

In fast- to medium-paced rivers chub respond well to longtrotting tactics, with the float set to present the bait just above bottom in conjunction with loosefed hookbait fragments – maggots, casters, worms, sweetcorn, wheat, breadflake or crust. In sluggish, coloured rivers, fish the waggler with small baits such as casters or maggots while loosefeeding the same or stewed hempseed. In really fast water or in low temperatures, quivertip ledger a static bait with cheese paste, worm or breadflake on the hook while feeding mashed bread. A block-end feeder/maggot or caster combination also scores well. Go down to small hooks for chub in popular fisheries.

Chunks of floating breadcrust or wasp-nest cake produce action in really weedy rivers during the summer, as do floating plugs. Small spinners, livebaits or wobbled deadbaits are readily accepted, both summer and winter.

Large, bushy dry flies like a sedge or mayfly will take chub from the surface, as will the daddy-longlegs. Wet flies and leaded nymphs work well, too. In warm weather, naturals such as a big lobworm or fat slug freelined through clear runs produce confident takes throughout the summer and autumn. Clear-water chub feed more confidently during the hours of darkness.

To extract the largest, heaviest, most cautious chub of all, those which clearly refuse even the most tempting baits offered during the hours of daylight, fishing after dark is the greatest leveller. Sea trout are in the very same league, and simply will not grab hold during daylight in low, clear water conditions, whatever the fly.

Really, the secret in fooling this wily species, particularly during the months of summer and autumn, is literally to spend more hours in location, with or without a rod, whilst wearing polaroid glasses, to gain intimate knowledge of the exact whereabouts of every shoal or individual specimens.

Make no mistake, if a chub has not an inkling of your presence, and your hookbait has been presented naturally on a free line, old rubber lips will usually gobble it up. Even relatively coarse tackle, will rarely be refused so long as it feels confident.

Torpedo-shaped, the chub has large scales in an even pattern, brassy flanks with a dark grey dorsal and tail, pale pinky-orange pelvic and anal fins, and a large mouth with thick-rimmed lips.

DACE

(Leuciscus leuciscus)

HABITAT

Dace are a river shoal fish and few stillwaters contain them. Although they tolerate coloured water and even shoal up in good numbers in deep, sluggish rivers, this species much prefers shallow, clear, weedy rivers, brooks and streams. In large river systems, dace reside in the clear, sparkling shallows immediately below weir- and mill-pools, the places where ditches and carrier streams enter the main river, overshoot pools, and so on, where they can often be seen darting over the clean gravel chasing aquatic flies that hatch in the surface film.

DISTRIBUTION

The dace has been introduced into and is spreading throughout selected rivers in southern Ireland, but is absent from most of Wales and Scotland. Throughout the whole of England there is scarcely a river system that does not contain dace, the largest being found in southern chalkstream trout fisheries such as the River Test and the upper reaches of the Kennet.

PHYSICAL CHARACTERISTICS

By far the smallest of the UK's 'catchable' species, the silvery dace is easily recognizable by its slim, smooth, rounded body, neat head and small mouth. Colouring is olive-grey along the back, changing to pewter. The flanks are covered with small, highly reflective silver scales. The belly is matt white.

The dace has pert, translucent fins with a touch of pale, yellowy-pink in the anal, pelvics and pectorals only. The tail is deeply forked. The dorsal and anal fins curve inwards, which easily distinguishes it from the chub, whose dorsal and anal fins are nicely rounded.

REPRODUCTION

Dace spawn in the spring, usually during April, among the shallowest areas of fast water over clean gravel. The pinkish, translucent eggs are deposited, usually after dark (probably to avoid the attention of predatory birds). The eggs may take two to three weeks to hatch.

EUROPEAN NAMES

FRANCE	Vandoise	HOLLAND	Serpeling
GERMANY	Hasel	SWEDEN	Stäm

WEIGHT RANGE

Average size:	2-6 oz (56-170 g)
Specimen size:	12 oz (340 g)
Record dace:	1 lb 4¼ oz (574 g) caught by J.L. Gasson, Little Ouse, Thetford, 1960.

Dace have delicate, smooth, rounded features, an even pattern of muted silver scales, a small, neat head and mouth and a forked, pale grey tail. The lower fins of the dace have a pinkish tint.

and the hatching fly, plus shrimps and other minute crustacea.

The wiry males are covered in tiny spawning tubercles and are rather sandpapery to the touch – a phenomenon noticeable to anglers during the months of February and March, when there is an apparent segregation of the sexes prior to the start of spawning.

FEEDING

When it comes to sucking in an imitation dry fly from the surface, dace are the quickest of biters. They can also suck in and blow out – having removed the inner juices with their pharyngeal teeth – maggot or a single caster with equal speed, but dace are not against chewing on a big worm or a large lump of paste. Their natural diet consists of all forms of aquatic insect life – nymphs, pupae

FISHING FOR DACE

During the warmer months, dace readily accept floating casters presented on a surface float rig, or baits such as maggots, casters, stewed wheat, breadcrust, offered at virtually any depth between the surface and the river bed. In cold, clear water, trot maggots or casters just above bottom while loosefeeding with the same, stewed hempseed or tares. When the river runs mucky or is in full flood, present the bait hard on the bottom with the float attached at both ends and set well over depth, stret-pegging style. Alternatively, in distant, deep or fast water, quivertip ledger using a blockend feeder/caster or maggot combination with small hooks and a fine hooklength.

Dace are great fun on the fly rod. They will accept standard wet flies fished downstream and across, or a slow-sinking or leaded nymph or shrimp presented upstream, but are most exciting on the dry fly. Small patterns are best on size 16, 18 hooks: try the Black Gnat, Greenwells Glory or Coachman.

EEL

(Anguilla anguilla)

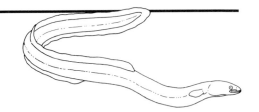

HABITAT

Eels love dark hideouts where they can hole up during bright daylight conditions. They burrow into soft silt or dense weedbeds and hide beneath large pieces of bottom debris. They occupy crevices beneath steep banking, locks, weirs, submerged tree roots, old boat-houses and bridge supports. In fact, any dark hideout on the bottom is liable to contain eels in both still and running water.

DISTRIBUTION

Eels are common in all river systems throughout the British Isles, and in most reservoirs, lakes, meres and gravel pit complexes. They even find their way into the most remote and tiniest of ponds that are not in any way connected to ditches or streams, by travelling overland across fields and lanes at night during heavy and prolonged rain.

PHYSICAL CHARACTERISTICS

On a weight for length basis, and reaching over 4 ft (1.2 m), the eel is by far the lightest of the UK's freshwater fish, and is impossible to confuse with

EUROPEAN NAMES

FRANCE	Anguille	SWEDEN	Ål
GERMANY	Aal	DENMARK	Ål
HOLLAND	Paling	SPAIN	Anguila
ITALY	Anguilla		

WEIGHT RANGE

Average size:	8 oz-1½ lb (225-680 g)
Specimen size:	Over 3½-4 lb (1.55-1.8 kg)
Record eel:	11 lbs 2 oz (5.468 kg) caught by S. Terry, Kingfisher Lakes, Hampshire, 1978.

C Turnbull 93

any other. It has a long, incredibly supple body, round in cross-section, but which compresses laterally towards the tail, and a comparatively small, neat head. The jaws are strong and lined with the tinest of whisker-like teeth. Its scales, which are minute and can only be seen through a magnifying glass, are covered in a thick layer of protective slime, or mucus.

The dorsal fin starts approximately one-third of the way down the back and continues around the tail, finishing halfway along its underside in front of the vent. It is, in fact, one continuous frill comprising dorsal, tail and anal fin. Pelvic fins are absent, but the eel sports neat pectoral fins immediately behind the gill opening. Colouring is a uniform green, or yellowy brown on top fusing into a noticeably lighter belly. These are known as either green or yellow eels and refer to the eel's colouring throughout most of its existence in fresh

water. The colour changes drastically, however, once adult eels feel the irrepressible urge to return to the sea to spawn after several years in fresh water. The body then loses all hint of green and yellow, turning into muted, metallic shades of grey and silver.

REPRODUCTION

Mass migrations of 'silver' eels occur throughout the late summer and autumn, but odd groups will run to sea during especially high water levels at virtually any time of the year. Certain phases of the moon are known to affect this downriver passage, which finds the eel making an arduously long journey across the Atlantic and down into the depths of the Sargasso Sea, where spawning takes place.

The fry start life incredibly thin and leaf-shaped. They can spend up to three years drifting with the

wind and tide in an easterly direction with the Gulf Stream towards UK shores, where they then shrink into glass eels or elvers prior to migrating upriver by the millions into fresh water during the late spring. A small percentage never enter fresh water, however, preferring to spend their lives in wide estuaries and in the sea proper.

FEEDING

Whether caught in the sea or in fresh water, eels are ravenous feeders. They consume all forms of aquatic insect larvae, worms, shrimps, snails, crayfish, amphibians and small live fish, and will happily gorge upon the carcasses of dead fish and mammals lying on the bottom. Eels feed most aggressively and are particularly active during the hours of darkness, and in the daytime when light values drop to a low level, such as during thunder storms.

FISHING FOR EEL

The easiest way of catching small to medium-sized eels – say, up to 1½ lb (680 g) in weight – is by offering a moving animal bait presented hard on the bottom. It should be either ledgered or laid on with float tackle. Use baits such as a bunch of maggots or brandlings, or a big, fat, juicy lobworm. Eels also like smelly baits such as cheesepaste, luncheon meat, squid, and small, freshly killed fish – minnows, gudgeons and dace. Large eels are nowhere near as suicidal as small ones, and can be put off by any undue resistance they feel when taking the bait. Eels are rarely caught once low winter temperatures set in.

The eel has a protruding lower jaw, and a long, slim, smooth, slimy body, round in cross-section with a continuous frill along the back and underneath, comprising dorsal, anal fin and tail.

FLOUNDER

(Platichthys flesus)

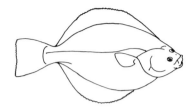

HABITAT

Though technically a shoaling sea fish, infant flounders migrate high up into fresh water, and only return to the sea where they were born after three or four years in order to spawn themselves. Weir-pools, in particular, are prime holding areas, and fast gravel or sandy runs are sometimes paved with this unusual fish.

DISTRIBUTION

Flounders travel upstream into the non-tidal waters of most river systems within the British Isles.

PHYSICAL CHARACTERISTICS

The flounder has a classic, flat-fish shape with a compressed body. Both eyes are situated on top next to the bony mouth. They are normally 'right sided', that is to say, with the eyes situated on the right, but left-handed flounders are not uncommon. The dorsal fin fringes almost the entire length of the body. The anal fin is noticeably shorter, with a pair of diminutive pelvic fins in front. The tail is square. The curved lateral line follows the contour of the pectoral fin.

The upper body is mainly grey, with a well-camouflaged arrangement of large, dark brown blotches, plus small brown and yellow spots. The underside is a plain, dull white. The flounder has a line of sharp denticles along the lateral line and the base of both long fins, which distinguishes it from other similar flatfish.

REPRODUCTION

Flounders spawn at sea in deep water during the spring. The fry change from a classic fish to the flat-fish shape within days of hatching, whereupon they sink to the bottom and remain there.

FEEDING

Flounders hunt worms, cockles and shrimps at sea; they feed mostly upon aquatic insect life and crustacea in rivers, although many an angler has his maggot or worm bait gobbled up.

EUROPEAN NAMES

FRANCE	Flet	HOLLAND	Bot
GERMANY	Flunder	SWEDEN	Skrubb-skädda

WEIGHT RANGE

Average size:	8-10 in (20-25 cm) long
Specimen size:	Over 2 lb (900 g)
Record flounder:	5 lb 3 oz 10 dr (2.370 kg) caught by M. R. Burgess, River Teign, Devon, 1987.

FISHING FOR FLOUNDERS

They are obliging biters to small, ledgered baits such as harbour ragworms, cockles, peeler crab, shrimps and prawns. They also respond aggressively to a plain white or silver 2-in (5-cm) special flounder spoon, the single hook of which should be baited with ragworm and worked slowly along the bottom, so it sends up tiny bursts of sand.

A curved lateral line follows the contour of the flounder's pectoral fin. A line of denticles runs along the lateral line and at the base of continuous fins on both side of the body.

GOLDFISH

(Carassius auratus)

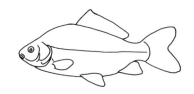

HABITAT

The goldfish does not live happily in running water or in unprotected, crystal-clear water due to its obvious attraction to predatory fish and birds such as the heron. It likes small, warm-water ponds, pits and lakes, where it will breed freely and successfully in green water, or among an entanglement of soft weeds and lily-pads.

DISTRIBUTION

Imported during the 17th century, goldfish and its numerous variants are now well established in both ornamental ponds and even isolated natural or wild stillwaters throughout the British Isles.

PHYSICAL CHARACTERISTICS

It has a typical carp-like body with a small, neat mouth. The overall body colour can vary from white, gold, yellow or red, or combinations of any two, to its original (wild form) olive-brown. In the case of the latter, is is often confused with small common or crucian carp. Goldfish, however, do not have barbels like common carp. And unlike the crucian, which has a rounded dorsal fin, that of the goldfish is concave, with a serrated first spine. Although in its original form the goldfish is fully scaled, part-scaled, scatter-scaled and virtually scale-less mutations have been created through selective breeding.

REPRODUCTION

It is the most interbred of all domesticated cyprinids, resulting in several decorative, exotic forms with particular fin and colour characteristics, such as fantails, shubunkins, comets, lionheads and blackmoors. It breeds during high water temperatures in June or July, when the males (often several at a time) can be seen chasing a swollen-bellied female through surface plants. Milt from the male is simultaneously released to fertilize the pinkish, translucent eggs, which adhere to soft weeds or the stems of marginal plants. Where such plants do not exist, submerged branches are used.

EUROPEAN NAMES			
FRANCE	Poisson Rouge	ITALY	Carassio Dorato
GERMANY	Goldfisch	SWEDEN	Gullfisk
HOLLAND	Goudvis	DENMARK	Guldfisk

WEIGHT RANGE

Average size: 2-4 oz (56-115 g). Can grow to over 2 lb (900 g).

The fry are usually drab brown in colour, but change to various shades of gold or red some time during their first two years. Some, however, never change, and retain the natural olive-brown pigmentation of their Eastern Asian ancestors throughout their entire life.

The goldfish sometimes interbreeds with crucian carp.

FEEDING

Goldfish feed on all forms of aquatic insect life, zooplankton and soft plant tissue, but are easily weaned onto the pelleted foods made from a fish meal and cereal base used by aquarium and pond enthusiasts.

FISHING FOR GOLDFISH

The species responds to most small baits used for other cyprinid species – maggots, worms, sweetcorn and breadflake or paste. It bites boldly on light float tackle, especially when the bait is suspended well above bottom. Use size 16-14 hooks direct to a 2 lb (900 g) test reel line. It is generally only caught by accident, but nevertheless gives a good account of itself.

Goldfish have many varied, even multicoloured and scatter scale-forms in red, orange, gold, yellow, white, black or blue. They have a concave dorsal with a serrated first spine and small, neat mouth.

GRAYLING

(Thymallus thymallus)

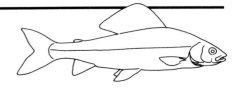

HABITAT

The grayling does not tolerate anything but pure, clean water high in dissolved oxygen. It exists in a few deep, clear, stream-fed lakes in southern England, but is most at home in bubbly, fast-flowing gravel and sandy-bottomed rivers.

DISTRIBUTION

This species is rather localized. It is most prolific in Scottish rivers and the chalkstreams of Hampshire and Berkshire. It is absent from Ireland.

PHYSICAL CHARACTERISTICS

It is impossible to confuse the grayling with any other species. It has a distinctive smell of thyme. Its long, wiry body is covered in small, flat-lying scales, and it has a neat head with underslung mouth and protruding top jaw. Adults are deeper and thicker across the shoulders. Colouring is dark grey-pewter along the back fusing into sides of dull pewter (sometimes with a mauve tinge), and it is liberally flecked with small, dark spots.

EUROPEAN NAMES

FRANCE	Ombre	ITALY	Temulo
GERMANY	Äsche	SWEDEN	Harr
HOLLAND	Vlagsalm	DENMARK	Stalling

WEIGHT RANGE

Average size:	6 oz-1¼ lb (170-560 g)
Specimen size:	Over 2 lb (900 g)
Record grayling:	4 lb 3 oz (1.899 kg) caught by S. R. Lanigan, River Frome, Dorset, 1989.

Chris Turnbull
93

The distinction between the sexes is made easy by the noticeably larger, sail-like dorsal fin of the male. The dorsals of both sexes, however, are exquisitely painted with lines of blue-black blotches between the rays and a fringe of scarlet along the top. It has a small, ray-less adipose fin, and a forked tail. The colourful pelvic and anal fins have a brown, horizontal mark between them, and there is a spot of the same colour on each side of the throat.

REPRODUCTION

Grayling mass on the gravelly shallows for spawning in the spring, during April, when the males become very territorial. Milt is shed over the eggs released by the female when she lowers her body into the gravel bottom. The eggs fall down between the stones, and hatch some 20-25 days later.

FEEDING

It is an aggressive, swift-moving feeder that will rise to feed on hatching flies in addition to taking all forms of bottom-dwelling aquatic insect life, shrimps, snails, and the eggs and fry of other fish. Adult grayling also prey upon small fish such as minnows.

FISHING FOR GRAYLING

Grayling respond to animal baits such as redworms or maggots longtrotted just above bottom through fast, even-paced runs. Use a buoyant, easy-to-see float carrying plenty of shot grouped 12 in (30 cm) above a size 14-12 hook tied direct to 2½ lb (1.1 kg) test. Loosefeed regularly and keep on the move, exploring all likely runs, especially those at the tail end of weir races, mini hatch pools and so on, in depths of 1-6 ft (30 cm-2 m), no matter how fast the flow. Hold the float back every so often to swing the bait upwards enticingly. The grayling bites boldly, and is a strong fighter. It raises its sail-like dorsal fin when it surfaces.

Grayling is great fun on the fly rod, hitting traditional wet-fly patterns fished downstream and across. It also accepts upstream nymph or leaded shrimp, and readily sucks in small dry-fly patterns. It leaves a distinctive, unmistakable 'ring' on the surface after it rises and returns to the bottom.

Smelling of thyme, the grayling's wiry, pewter-grey body is liberally flecked with black spots. Males have a huge sail-like dorsal; the female's is much smaller and squared. Grayling have a protruding top lip.

GUDGEON

(Gobio gobio)

HABITAT
Like barbel, the gudgeon is a bottom-living fish that prefers and is most prolific in rivers, where it masses in large shoals (often of hundreds, even thousands strong) in the swift-flowing shallows wherever the bottom consists of clean sand or gravel. Gudgeon also fair well in stillwaters, gravel pits in particular.

DISTRIBUTION
Gudgeon are common in the majority of river systems throughout the British Isles, with the exception of Scotland.

PHYSICAL CHARACTERISTICS
Though having the classic wedge-shaped head and snout, gudgeon are immediately identified and easily distinguished from other barbel-like bottom-dwellers by their two whiskers or barbels; one situated each side of the semi-protrusible mouth. The barbel, of course, has four whiskers and the loach no less than six.

Gudgeon are also thicker set and rather higher in the back than related species, but possess the same cylindrical body tapering rapidly towards a forked tail.

Colouring, which overall often suggests a speckled 'blueness', varies from light brown to pewter along the back, fusing into dull silver below the distinct lateral line, along which are up to a dozen dark (blueish) blotches. Rows of small, dark markings or flecks cover the fins – a characteristic shared with the loach, but not the barbel.

REPRODUCTION
Some time in late May or during June, the female gudgeon releases her eggs over a clean gravel bottom. These are immediately fertilized by a spray of milt, often from more than one male. The sticky eggs adhere to stones or weeds such as willow moss, where they hatch some 10-12 days later. Initially the tiny fry are almost invisible, but their colouring becomes more distinct with age.

FEEDING
Gudgeon consume shrimps, midge larvae, mayfly nymphs, water louse, caddis grubs and annelid worms. They are voracious feeders, especially when present in large shoals and competition is strong.

EUROPEAN NAMES

FRANCE	Goujon	ITALY	Gobione
GERMANY	Gründling	SWEDEN	Sandkry-
HOLLAND	Rivier-		pare
	grondel	DENMARK	Grundling

WEIGHT RANGE

Average size:	Up to 1 oz (28 g), 3-5 in (7.5-12.5 cm) long
Specimen size:	2 oz (55 g) plus
Record gudgeon:	5 oz (141 g) caught by D. H. Hull, River Nadder, Wiltshire, 1990.

FISHING FOR GUDGEON

Gudgeon do not like chasing their food, preferring it to be presented on or within 1-2 in (2.5-5 cm) of the bottom, whether floatfished or ledgered. Offered on hooks in sizes 16 to 20, the best baits include maggots, casters and punched bread, while match fishermen take enormous hauls of gudgeon using bloodworm (midge larvae). Tiny redworms or brandling are also good bait. Owing to its erratic, attractive swimming motion, the gudgeon makes a great livebait for zander, perch and eels.

The gudgeon has a wedge-shaped head, two whiskers (barbel have four and loach six), speckled blue blotches along the flanks, and a forked tail.

STONE LOACH

(Noemacheilus barbatulus)

HABITAT
While this, the most common European loach, prefers clear-flowing ditches, brooks, sidestreams and rivers, where it hides beneath large stones, flints or overhanging banks, it can tolerate even stagnant and slow-moving water low in dissolved oxygen.

DISTRIBUTION
The stone loach is common in most river systems throughout the British Isles, except for the north of Scotland.

PHYSICAL CHARACTERISTICS
It has a wiry, barbel-like shape with an exceptionally smooth, slippery body covered in minute scales. Its flattened, wedge-shaped head with underslung mouth sports six barbels or whiskers. Four sprout from the top lip, with one at each corner of the mouth. The fins are square, slightly rounded at the corners and flecked in rows of dark markings. The overall body colouring is an olive brown, mottled with irregular dark blotches. The stone loach has the ability to supplement its oxygen intake by rising to the surface and gulping in air, which passes through the intestine and is released via the anus.

FEEDING
The stone loach consumes all types of aquatic insect larvae and shrimps, which it locates by grubbing about amongst the sand and gravel with its armoury of sensory whiskers.

FISHING FOR STONE LOACH
While schoolboys set out to catch loach in handnets or on light float tackle baited with small worms, they are rarely caught by ardent anglers. Stone loach are very resilient little fish and thus make great livebaits for predators like perch and chub. They are easily gathered from ditches and sidestreams by holding an aquarium-type, fine-mesh net tightly against the bottom immediately

EUROPEAN NAMES			
FRANCE	**Loche**	ITALY	**Cobite**
	Franche	SWEDEN	**Grönling**
GERMANY	**Schmerle**	DENMARK	**Smerling**

WEIGHT RANGE
Average size: 2½-5 in (5-12.5 cm) long

downstream of any large flint or stone. The loach then swim straight into the net when the stone is gently raised. Hook one once only with a size 4 or 6 hook through both nostrils and suspend it beneath a float, or freeline it through weedy runs or deep gullies with just a single swan shot on the lne 12 in (30 cm) above the hook.

NOTE
There is also a smaller species of loach, called the spined loach (*Cobitis taenia*), which is recognisable by the tiny erect spine set in a groove below each eye. Its distribution is limited to localized areas of England only.

The stone loach has a mottled, olive-brown, smooth, wiry body, an underslung mouth sporting six whiskers, and a squared tail. All the fins are flecked with dark markings.

MINNOW

(Phoxinus phoxinus)

HABITAT

The minnow is the UK's smallest cyprinid shoal fish. It likes the bubbly, well-oxygenated, clear-flowing, shallow water of brooks, streams and large rivers. It also inhabits stream-fed, pure-water lakes and gravel pits.

DISTRIBUTION

The minnow is common on the fast, gravelly shallows of most river systems throughout the British Isles, and is thus a good barometer of water quality.

PHYSICAL CHARACTERISTICS

Slim, rounded, and smooth to the touch with the tiniest of scales, the minnow has a small mouth, but comparatively large eyes. It is grey-brown along the back, with a broken line of olive-brown markings along the mid flank from the gill plate to the tail. The tail is forked and has a dark blotch at the root. The belly is silvery white, and the fins are rounded and translucent grey.

REPRODUCTION

Spawning occurs during May or June, the eggs being laid *en masse* on the gravel bottom. At this time the males noticeably colour up, sporting a flash of red on their lips and bellies, with a cover-

With smooth, rounded features and a large eye, the minnow's body is barred horizontally in a line of olive-bronze markings. It has a silvery white belly.

ing of tiny white spawning tubercles over their heads and shoulders.

FEEDING

Minnows eat all small forms of aquatic insect, crustacea and worms.

FISHING FOR MINNOWS

While schoolboys deliberately set out to catch minnows, serious fishermen often find them a nuisance during the summer, when they greedily suck in trotted maggots intended for larger species. Minnows do, however, make a superb natural bait for predators such as perch, chub, trout and barbel, whether trotted close to the bottom beneath a chunky float, or tapped on the head and ledgered as a mini deadbait. Hook one gently through both nostrils with a size 6 hook tied direct to 5-6 lb (2.25-2.7 kg) line.

EUROPEAN NAMES			
FRANCE	Vairon	SWEDEN	Kvidd
GERMANY	Elritze	DENMARK	Elrits
HOLLAND	Emmerling		
ITALY	Sangui-nerola		

WEIGHT RANGE

Average size: 2-3 in (5-7.5 cm)
Record minnow: 13 dr (23 g) caught by R. Merrifield, River Calder, Nelson, Lancs, 1981.

MULLET

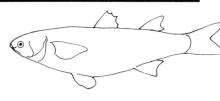

THIN-LIPPED GREY MULLET
(Liza ramada)

THICK-LIPPED GREY MULLET
(Chelon labrosus)

GOLDEN GREY MULLET
(Liza auratus)

HABITAT

The mullet is a shoaling sea fish that spends much of its life close inshore, in estuaries, around piers and in harbours beneath boats, and especially around the discharge pipes of sewerage and waste food. The thin-lipped grey mullet also runs high up into rivers, sometimes in huge shoals, spending the summer and autumn months entirely in fresh water.

DISTRIBUTION

It is common around the entire coastline of the British Isles, entering all estuaries and rivers.

PHYSICAL CHARACTERISTICS

Although three species are found in British coastal waters, the differences are slight. Their overall shape is like a torpedo, similar to chub and grass carp, while the eye is set unusually low – level with the jaw hinge – just like the grass carp's. The most striking, instantly recognizable feature of all three species is that mullet have two separate dorsal fins, both of equal size. The first contains four spikes, the second is of soft rays. Only the bass shares this feature, but its first dorsal contains eight or nine spines, so there's no chance of confusion. Mullet also has a prickly leading edge to its pelvic fins.

Colouring varies from sandy brown to pewter, to blue-grey along the back. Along the silvery flanks are four to six rows of scales that are high-lighted with dark grey lines, though these stripes are sometimes completely missing, particularly in young mullet.

The fins are translucent grey and the tail is deeply forked. The thick-lipped grey mullet

EUROPEAN NAMES			
FRANCE	**Muge**	HOLLAND	**Harder**
GERMANY	**Meerasche**	ITALY	**Cephalo**

WEIGHT RANGE

Average size:	1-2 lb (450-900 g)
Specimen size:	Over 5 lb (2.25 kg) for thick-lipped; over 3 lb (1.35 kg) for thin-lipped
Record (thick-lipped) grey mullet:	14 lb 2¾ oz (6.427 kg) caught by R. S. Gifford, Aberthan, Glamorgan, Wales, 1979.

has lips twice as thick as the thin-lipped variety, which has a tell-tale dark base to the root of its pectoral fins. The golden grey mullet gets its name from the golden spot in the middle of its gill cover, sometimes accompanied by a golden sheen along the flanks. Otherwise this smallest species closely resembles the thin-lipped mullet.

REPRODUCTION
Mullet spawn in the sea and in the mouths of estuaries in the spring, laying eggs that float.

FEEDING
Mullet eat all manner of tiny organisms and organic matter including crustacea and molluscs, soft weeds, filamentous algae and large quantities

of soft bottom mud. Their 'feeding' lip marks can easily be identified on the mudflats when the tide is out.

FISHING FOR MULLET

Mullet can be the most frustrating of all fish to catch. Some days they won't bite at any price. On other occasions they can be attracted using freshwater-style groundbaits such as mashed bread, or even floating crust, which they will eventually suck in during spells of heatwave weather. Alternatively, try a blood-based groundbait called shirvy. Simply mince up extremely fine quantities of meat or fish, and add some fish oil, blood and bran (to bind it all together). Every so often, flick in a tablespoon of shirvy, and wait for the tide to bring a shoal of mullet up to you.

Floatfishing with a chubber or loafer float to a 4 lb (1.8 kg) reel line and 13 or 14 ft (3.96 or 4.26 m) match rod is the way to catch mullet. Use small hooks in sizes 14-10 tied direct, and place the shots well away from the bait, allowing it to sway naturally in the current. Try thin slivers of raw steak or fish strip, fragments of harbour ragworm, sweetcorn or breadflake. And be prepared for an exciting, fast and powerful tussle. Mullet can also be tempted with a really tiny spinner baited with ragworm fragments.

This fish is a thin-lipped grey mullet. The thick-lipped variety has noticeably thicker lips. The golden grey mullet has a golden spot on its gill cover.

GOLDEN ORFE

(Leuciscus idus var. Auratus

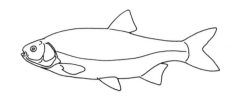

HABITAT

The golden orfe likes a clean, clear, weedy environment in either still or running water, where it is forever on the move close to the surface, ready to suck in aquatic nymphs as they rise, hatching flies, or terrestrial flies landing on the surface.

DISTRIBUTION

It has a scattered existence in a handful of rivers in southern England, but is becoming more widespread as an angling fish throughout the British Isles in modern, man-made fisheries.

EUROPEAN NAMES

NONE

WEIGHT RANGE

Average size:	¾-1½ lb (337-680 kg)
Specimen size:	2½-3 lb (1.1-1.35 kg)
Record golden orfe:	5 lb 5 oz (2.,409 kg)
	caught by M. Battersby,
	Lymmvale, Cheshire, 1990.

PHYSICAL CHARACTERISTICS

It is similar to an outsize dace in body shape, with smooth, rounded features and a small mouth. Also, just like the dace, it can only be sexed during spawning, when the males turn sandpapery to the touch due to the tiny spawning tubercles that appear on their heads and shoulders.

It has a distinct overall colouring of peachy-orange along the back and flanks, often flecked with the occasional dark blotch, fusing into a belly of muted silver. All the fins are also orange, often with a rosy tint, and the tail is deeply forked.

The 'ide' (*Leuciscus idus*) common throughout Europe is, in fact, the 'wild orfe', a neutral-coloured fish from which the golden variety (and a blue variant) has been derived. It is much like a giant dace, with a deeper body and brassy-buttery flanks.

REPRODUCTION

Golden orfe spawn during April or early May, depositing their eggs in shallow water over stones or fibrous marginal vegetation, such as willow roots or willow moss. In stillwaters it is most likely to spawn at the entrances of streams or inlet pipes, where flowing water creates a higher level of dissolved oxygen. The fry hatch after 16-20 days, and initially feed upon phyto, and then zooplankton.

FEEDING

It feeds at all levels, but is more active near the surface in the warm upper water layers, where it loves to dart about quickly, sucking in falling or floating items of natural food.

FISHING FOR GOLDEN ORFE

Best results are achieved by presenting small, floating baits like casters or cubes of breadcrust (in conjunction with loosefeed) on a flat float rig, or with the aid of a controller if you are distance fishing. Orfe also take baits such as maggots, flake or sweetcorn readily on the drop, but bite with lightning speed and immediately reject the bait if they feel undue resistance. Use hook sizes 16-12 tied direct to 2 lb (900 g) test. The orfe is not a particularly strong or exciting fighter, but specimens do represent a most colourful, difficult challenge. In clear water they are frustrating to catch.

Dace-like in shape with smooth, rounded features and painted in peachy-orange, the golden orfe can never be confused with other species.

PERCH

(Perca fluviatilis)

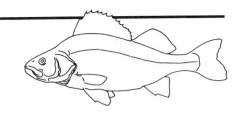

HABITAT

Lovers of both still and running water, perch prefer to live close to, beneath or among structures like wooden pilings and boat-houses, sunken trees, deep holes and gullies, and road and railway bridges spanning rivers. They are happiest surrounded by the vertical stems of marginal plants such as tall reeds and bullrushes, where their vertical bars blend in marvellously, offering protection from predators, yet providing camouflage – enabling them to pounce upon small shoal fish that pass by.

DISTRIBUTION

The perch is found throughout the British Isles in the majority of lowland river systems and particularly in gravel pits, ponds, lakes, meres, broads and reservoirs. Small, man-made irrigation reservoirs are especially favoured. Perch are prolific throughout southern Ireland in all lakes and river systems.

PHYSICAL CHARACTERISTICS

The perch has a deep, hump-backed body when adult, with between six and nine dark, vertical bars along golden olive flanks. The pelvic and lower half of the tail fin are coloured in bright orange-scarlet red. The pectoral is set high up against the gill cover and is virtually colourless. The fish has a double dorsal fin: the first is strongly spined with a dark blotch at the base of the last two spines, the second has soft rays. Its belly is silvery white.

Check for a large, expandable, bony mouth with bristles on the tongue and bristle-gripping pads in the throat. Scales are rough to the touch. Colouring becomes more intense in clear, weedy waters, and rather drab in heavily coloured waters.

There can be few baits, natural or man-made, which turn perch into a feeding mood more effectively than the humble lobworm, whether presented static on the bottom or twitched erratically through the swim.

EUROPEAN NAMES			
FRANCE	**Perche**	SWEDEN	**Abbore**
GERMANY	**Barsch**	DENMARK	**Abore**
HOLLAND	**Baars**	SPAIN	**Perca**
ITALY	**Perca**		

WEIGHT RANGE

Average size:	**4-12 oz (115-350 g)**
Specimen size:	**Over 2 lb (900 g)**
Record perch:	**5 lb 9 oz (2.608 kg)**
	caught by Mr J. Shayler,
	Furnace Pond, Kent, 1985.

REPRODUCTION

Perch spawn early – usually during April – laying strings of sticky white eggs through reed stems, over sunken branches and fibrous tree roots in the marginal shallows. The goggle-eyed fry hatch within 8-9 days.

FEEDING

Infant perch start with animal plankton, shrimps and aquatic insect larvae, but quickly move on to a diet comprising mostly small fish of all species, including their own kind. Self-cropping is, in fact, responsible for fisheries containing only two or three year classes of perch – very small and very large specimens.

FISHING FOR PERCH

Perch readily respond to floatfished animal baits, particularly worms, maggots and casters, presented in the lower water layers close to the bottom. Ledgered lobworms, small, live and even freshly killed small fish, minnows, gudgeon and small perch, are the best method for producing the larger specimens occupying deep water. Floatfished, free-roaming, small livebaits work well in shallow, even-depth stillwaters, while in selected deep areas, gravel-pit gullies, holes on the bends of a river and weir-pools the paternostered livebait is recommended.

This fish responds to all methods of artificial lure fishing - even flies. Large, gaudy fry imitation patterns like the Dog Nobbler, account for prolific catches of perch from large trout reservoirs. A light spinning tackle outfit using 0 to size 3 mepps, ondex, voblex spinners, and others, permits enjoyment from even modest-sized perch. Spoons and vibratory diving plugs also produce. The American-designed 'spinner bait' is particularly effective, even in coloured waters with low visibility, where the perch homes in on the lure's vibratory pulses. A bunch of worms added to the hook of an artificial lure sometimes encourages more hits.

Baited lines, spoons and spinners really do make perch hit with more aggression. They are immediately attracted to the pulsating vibrations of the artificial, but really hang on and for longer, to those baited with worms or a sliver of fresh fish strip.

The perch has scarlet-orange fins, double dorsals, the first heavily spined, bony jaws and six to nine dark vertical bars along its olive-green flanks.

PIKE

(Esox Lucius)

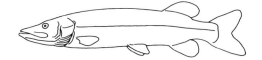

HABITAT

The pike exists happily everywhere, in all still and running waters except the fastest, rockiest of spate rivers. It relies on its marvellous body camouflage to ambush its prey while lying in wait among weed-

EUROPEAN NAMES

FRANCE	**Brochet**	SWEDEN	**Gadda**
GERMANY	**Hecht**	DENMARK	**Gedde**
HOLLAND	**Snoek**	SPAIN	**Lucio**
ITALY	**Luccio**		

WEIGHT RANGE

Average size:	**5-12 lb (2.25-5.45 kg)**
Specimen size:	**Over 20 lb (9 kg)**
Record pike:	**46 lb (20.884 kg) caught by R. Lewis, Llandegfedd Reservoir, 1992.**

beds, rush and reed beds, sunken trees and other obstacles. It also hunts shoal fish in open water at all depths, sucks up dead fish off the bottom, and attacks surface prey.

DISTRIBUTION

The pike is common throughout the British Isles in all river systems and in most stillwaters. Reservoirs, gravel pits and broads where fodder fish exist in large shoals breed pike in large numbers and of a high average size.

PHYSICAL CHARACTERISTICS

With its long, sleek body and large dorsal fin set

well back close to the tail, the pike is easily the most recognizable of all UK freshwater species. Vertical bars across the back fuse down the flanks into a mosaic of creamy white spots over olive green, which ends in line with the pelvic fin. The belly is creamy white. The large forked tail provides the sudden, explosive thrust used for a swift attack upon prey, and like all the fins it is mottled, often with a warm tinge.

The pike has large, strong jaws and a pointed snout. The lower jaw protrudes slightly in front of the upper one and contains several large, piercing teeth that are used for instantly immobilizing large items of prey. In the roof of the upper jaw are hundreds of tiny, backward-slanting teeth, ensuring that what goes in seldom comes out again.

The small scales are set flat to the body, protected by a liberal covering of strong-smelling mucus. The colouring of clear-water pike is far more intense than those in heavily coloured water, which often take on an overall sandy, yellow hue. The spotting pattern is different on each side, permitting individual pike that are caught regularly to be positively identified.

REPRODUCTION

Accompanied by up to three or four much smaller males (jacks), female pike move on to the shallows for spawning and to shed their eggs during the early spring – usually sometime in April – among reed and rush stems or submerged marginal vegetation. The eggs hatch within two weeks and the fry live in dense vegetation, feeding initially on invertebrates and aquatic insect larvae. However, when only inches long their diet quickly turns to the fry of other fish.

FEEDING

The pike is the most aggressive of freshwater fish. It preys on newts, toads, frogs and crayfish, and the young of waterbirds such as coots and moorhens (even a fully grown mallard is not totally safe), in addition to fish of all species, including its own kind.

Many a pike has been found dead, choked to death upon a meal that was far too big for its gullet.

FISHING FOR PIKE

Although pike will occasionally grab a twitched worm intended for perch or chub, chase a lump of fluffy white breadflake on the retrieve, or even hit

the fly fisherman's imitative fry patterns with a speed equal to any brown or rainbow trout, they succumb most readily to three techniques: worked artificial lures, livebaits and deadbaits.

Small spinners and spinning jigs produce great numbers of small to medium-sized pike, while a freshly killed deadbait – either natural or a sea fish such as herring, smelt or mackerel – presented

completely static on the bottom invariably produces a much larger stamp of pike, particularly from heavily coloured waters. Wobbled deadbaits also catch plenty of pike, including a few specimens, as will deadbaits mounted horizontally and worked beneath a sail-type drift float in strong winds. Overall, however, and taking all types of fishing into account, livebaiting (free-roaming or paternostered) is the most effective and consistent method of catching because it comes closest to imitating the pike's natural daily diet of live fish.

The pike's long, athletic, olive-green body is liberally covered by cream markings. The anal fin is set close to its large, forked tail, and with strong, teeth-laden jaws, there can be no possible confusion with it and other species.

PUMPKINSEED

(Lepomis gibbosus)

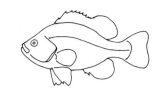

HABITAT

This colourful shoal fish fares especially well in small stillwaters such as ponds, pits and lakes that have prolific weed growth, and in canals.

DISTRIBUTION

The pumpkinseed is the smallest member of the American sun bass family, and was originally imported into the UK for the aquarist market because of its colourful appearance and durability. Having subsequently been released into the wild, it now flourishes in isolated stillwaters and canals throughout England.

PHYSICAL CHARACTERISTICS

The pumpkinseed is impossible to confuse with indigenous British species due to its deep, laterally compressed body and unusual markings: mottled turquoise blue and brown along the back and upper flank, suddenly changing to golden-orange on the belly and throat. It has a typical bass-like, protruding bottom jaw, and its double dorsal fin is continuous. The first dorsal is spined, the second made of soft rays. The leading edge of the anal fin is also spined.

REPRODUCTION

This species breeds in shallow water over fine sand or gravel during June and July. The male scoops out a depression in the bottom, and once the female has deposited her eggs in it he fertilizes them. He then stands guard throughout incubation, which takes up to a week, and afterwards until the shoal of fry vacate the nest.

FEEDING

The pumpkinseed is an aggressive, competitive shoal fish consuming all forms of aquatic insect larvae and crustacea, plus the spawn and fry of other fish. Being virtually at the bottom of the food chain, it becomes staple food itself for much larger predators such as big mouth bass, zander and pike and even a large perch.

EUROPEAN NAMES			
FRANCE	**Perche-soleil**	HOLLAND	**Zonnebaars**
GERMANY	**Sonnen-barsch**	ITALY	**Persico sole**

WEIGHT RANGE

Average size: **4-7 in (10-17.5 cm) long**
Record pumpkinseed: **4 oz 9 dr (129 g) caught by D. L. Wallis, Whessoe Pond, Darlington, Co. Durham, 1987.**

FISHING FOR PUMPKINSEED

The fish bites readily to small animal baits such as worms, maggots, mealworms and caddis grub presented off the bottom on light float tackle. Use a 2 lb (900 g) reel line with size 16-12 hooks tied direct, and encourage the shoal into competing by regularly introducing loosefed hookbait samples. It bites boldly, like all members of the sun bass family, of which there are over 20 separate species in North American fresh waters.

And like all these species, the pumpkinseed can also effectively be caught with a light fly fishing outfit. In shallow water a sink tip or floating line set up is perfect with a cast of no more than 2 lb (1 kg) test at the point.

Use artificials like the Montana stone, leaded shrimp, sedge pupa, etc, presented slowly sinking. If nothing grabs hold by the time the fly reaches its 'dangle point', gently twitch it back in an erratic retrieve, expecting a slamming take to come almost at any point from the bottom to the surface. Lightly leaded flies tied on size 12-16 hooks will induce more takes.

The pumpkinseed has a deep, mottled turquoise and bronze-green body, with a golden orange belly and throat. Males (bottom) are more coloured with a bright red spot on the gill cover. Note the protruding lower jaw.

ROACH

(Rutilus rutilus)

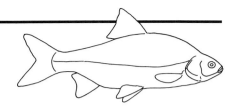

HABITAT

The roach is a shoal fish that thrives prolifically almost everywhere, from the tiniest of green-coloured ponds to clear-flowing chalkstreams. It attains its best ultimate weight within a lush environment both in stillwaters and in rivers of a slow to moderate pace, harbouring an abundant growth of soft, rooted plants. It also fares well in tidal rivers, where shoals are often numerically large, containing several hundred mature roach.

It likes weir-pools, mill-pools, deep runs, holes on the bends, deep, even-paced glides, confluences, shaded runs beneath overhanging trees, road and rail bridges – anything that provides cover. However, it also browses the bottom of deep, open waters such as reservoirs, estate lakes, meres, broads and gravel pits when grouped within the protection of a large shoal.

DISTRIBUTION

The most common and popular of all British freshwater species, roach are usually prolific in small, man-made lakes, ponds, pits, canals and slow-moving rivers. It is widely distributed, but absent from Scottish waters north of Perthshire. It is not endemic to Ireland, but having been introduced, it is now well established throughout the major river systems, both in the north and south.

PHYSICAL CHARACTERISTICS

The roach is the classic cyprinid shoal-fish shape. It has a small mouth, neat head and perfect, uniformly scaled body with a distinctive lateral line. It is oval in cross-section with a deepish body. Mature specimens from rich waters are often very deep in the body. Colouring along the back varies between grey-green and grey-brown, fusing down the sides into scales that give the effect of highly reflective enamel. During the warmer months roach are noticeably brassy along the flanks, yet once water temperatures drop, the scales show a definite winter blueness along the outer edges. The belly is matt white.

EUROPEAN NAMES			
FRANCE	**Gardon**	ITALY	**Scardola**
GERMANY	**Plötze**		**Coda Rossa**
HOLLAND	**Voorn**	SWEDEN	**Mort**
		DENMARK	**Skalle**

WEIGHT RANGE

Average size:	**4-10 oz (115-285 g)**
Specimen size:	**Over 2 lb (900 g)**
Record roach:	**4 lb 3 oz (1.842 kg)**
	caught by Mr Ray Clarke,
	Dorset Stour, 1990.

To be sure that a roach is a true roach and not a rudd, check that its warm, translucent grey-brown dorsal fin starts in a vertical line with the root of the pelvic fins, and when folded does not overlap the start of the anal fin. Its lips should be almost level when open, unlike the rudd, which has a protruding lower jaw, and the bream, whose vacuum-type mouth is fully protrusible.

The pectoral fin has a warm tinge, while the pelvics and anal both have much stronger tints of orange-red. The forked tail also has a noticeable warmth, particularly in mature specimens, which show a touch of crimson.

REPRODUCTION

Roach mass on the shallows during late spring – usually in May – often by the thousand, shedding their small, sticky yellow eggs on willow moss, on the fibrous matting of sub-surface tree roots, and on soft, rooted weeds. Within 10-12 days the eggs hatch, and the fry hug the weeds, feeding initially on a diet of minute vegetable plankton.

FEEDING

Roach consume all small forms of aquatic food, including insect larvae, shrimps, zooplankton and snails, plus a certain amount of plant tissue, particularly soft weeds. They are much affected by the

chain reaction of other shoal members during day-light hours, and they feed most aggressively during low light values at dawn and particularly as dusk falls.

FISHING FOR ROACH

Small to medium-sized roach readily accept small baits such as tares and stewed wheat, in addition to the more popular and commonly used maggots and casters, presented on light float tackle some-where between mid-water and the bottom. Specimen roach are more likely to accept a larger static bait such as a bunch of maggots, crust cube or breadflake presented hard on the bottom beneath a float at close range, or ledgered when fishing at a distance into stillwaters or deep, fast-

flowing rivers.

In cold conditions, when roach much prefer a small mouthful, quivertip ledger using a blockend feeder/maggot or caster combination. Long trotting on medium-paced rivers during periods of mild winter weather is a good way to locate the shoals, provided bait is set to trip just off bottom.

Roach is a popular species with match fishermen, who catch it most effectively using a carbon pole and full-length line (to hand) method. This works most effectively in deep water close in.

The roach has a small, neat mouth with lips almost level when open. The evenly scaled body has a distinct lateral line. Silver scales are edged in blue or brass, the belly is white and the fins warm.

ROACH/BREAM HYBRID

The roach/bream hybrid is by far the most common freshwater hybrid, and results from the two most common species simultaneously using the same spawning grounds. Eggs from the roach are fertilized by milt from a bream, or vice versa, producing a firm-bodied, hard-fighting roach/bream hybrid that is really neither one nor the other, but has characteristics of both species, although rarely on a 50/50 basis.

DISTINGUISHING FEATURES
Some hybrids will appear more bream-like with a semi-protrusible mouth and bronze flanks, but have noticeably large, roach-like scales, while others look distinctly roach-like in both shape and outline, but rather drab in body colour, lacking any warmth in the fins. Hybrids sometimes also have a dark outer rim on the dorsal and anal fins and tail, which, of course, true roach and bream do not. This is more pronounced in low water temperatures.

If you are still in doubt about an odd-looking roach, study the anal fin, which is always longer in a hybrid.

Hybrids regularly attain weights of 3-4 lb (1.35-1.8kg), with occasional specimens reaching 7 lb (3.15 kg). Sadly, at the present time, there is no classification for these fine fish under the British Record Fish List.

Less bronze than true bream, roach/bream hybrids lack the warmth in their fins. They have a longer anal fin than true roach, and have a slightly protruding mouth.

ROACH/RUDD HYBRID

This is by far the most difficult of all hybrids to identify. However, it is rather more common than the majority of fishermen realize because they often mistake it for either a slightly off-colour rudd or an extra-bright roach.

DISTINGUISHING FEATURES

As the true roach has lips that are almost level when open compared to the rudd's exaggerated protruding bottom lip, be immediately suspicious of a fish with a slightly protruding bottom lip – it is probably a hybrid. Hybrids also have a slight 'keel' to the anal fin, although it is not generally as pronounced as that of the true rudd, while the dorsal

The roach/rudd hybrid has slightly larger scales than a true roach with more warmth in the fins. The lower lip only slightly protrudes. The dorsal slightly overlaps the anal fin in a vertical line.

fin may be set only slightly further back than a true roach.

This hybrid is invariably slightly deeper in the body and more brassy along the flanks than a true roach, without that bright, buttery gold enamel of a true rudd. In addition, it rarely sports that winter blueness around the shoulders and along the back of the true roach. It also lacks the intense orange-scarlet fins of the true rudd.

RUDD

(Scardinius erythropthalmus)

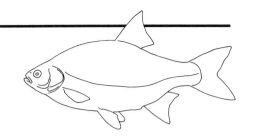

HABITAT

Rudd is a shoal fish that prefers a clear-water, weedy environment, especially those where the water has a 'peaty' tinge. It loves to feed in the upper layers, and is never far from cover such as reed lines, rush, and sedges, beds of lilies and broad-leaved potomogeton. Rudd also love submerged rooted plants like Canadian pondweed, milfoil and hornwort.

It thrives best of all in meres and estate lakes, the weedy shallow areas of well-established gravel pits, irrigation drains, canals, reservoirs and farm ponds.

In southern Ireland rudd are a prolific river and lake fish (as indeed they once were throughout many English river systems), because there the water quality has yet to be affected by excessive boating activity, sewerage effluent and farming chemicals.

DISTRIBUTION

Rudd is most prolific in southern Ireland, where it is more common than roach. It is rare in Scotland and much of Wales, but reasonably well spread throughout England, particularly in the Eastern counties of Norfolk, Suffolk, Lincolnshire and Cambridgeshire.

PHYSICAL CHARACTERISTICS

The rudd is deeper in the body than roach, but slimmer in cross-section. Its most noticeable and distinguishing feature is its protruding lower jaw, which is well designed for sucking in food from above.

The species is uniformly scaled in a burnished, highly reflective, buttery-gold enamel along the flanks, fusing upwards to an olive-bronze along the back. The belly is pale gold. Fins are orange-scarlet, the pelvics and anal being particularly bright. The anal fin is set on a rather sharp keel, and the dorsal is set much further back than that of the roach, actually overlapping the anal in a vertical line.

EUROPEAN NAMES

FRANCE	**Rotengle**	ITALY	**Scardola**
GERMANY	**Rotfeder**	SWEDEN	**Sarv**
HOLLAND	**Blankvoorn**	DENMARK	**Rudskalle**

WEIGHT RANGE

Average size:	**4-8 oz (115-225 g)**
Specimen size:	**Over 2 lb (900 g)**
Record rudd:	**4 lb 8 oz (2.410 kg) caught by Rev. E. C. Alston, a mere in Thetford, 1933.**

REPRODUCTION

Having gathered on the shallows in huge shoals during the late spring, rudd usually spawn in May. The translucent, pinkish eggs are distributed over any fibrous medium such as sub-surface tree roots, marginal rush and reed stems, grasses and rooted weeds, and hatch within two weeks. The fry feed at first on microscopic vegetable plankton, then on zoo plankton in the warmer surface layers.

FEEDING

Rudd feed on all aquatic insects, zooplankton, snails, shrimps and vegetable matter, and are particularly active close to the surface, sucking in the rising pupae of aquatic flies as they are about to hatch, and the newly hatched flies. Their splashy rises are a common sight on warm summer evenings. While small rudd are most obliging day-time feeders, adult rudd bite more boldly as dusk approaches and during the hours of darkness. They are often more difficult to catch during the cold winter months than roach. This is a rather strange phenomenon, generally relating to both small and medium-sized rudd only. The specimens, those stunning deep bodied beauties of 2 lb (1 kg) and more are not so lethargic in cold conditions and will respond to large ledgered baits quite aggressively.

FISHING FOR RUDD

In snaggy or weedy areas of stillwater during high summer, especially where both ledgering and float-fishing techniques are impossible, the ever-active rudd provides fabulous sport on the fly rod. Rudd readily accept slow-sinking nymphs (try the mayfly nymph, leaded shrimp and sedge pupae) and artificial dry flies. Patterns such as the Black Gnat, all the olives and small sedges work well.

Rudd respond quickly to surface baits such as casters and breadcrusts presented on a greased line with the flat float technique. Fishing on the drop with a small, slow-sinking offering – for instance maggots, casters, sweetcorn or stewed wheat – presented beneath a loaded dart, zoomer or waggler

Rudd have deep, evenly coloured, burnished, buttery-gold flanks, a protruding bottom jaw, and bright orange-scarlet pelvic and anal fins. The dorsal noticeably overlaps the anal fin in a vertical line.

float, catches rudd from the upper water layers.

Large ledgered baits – worms or breadflake – usually account for rudd of a much higher average size.

For the real whoppers, ledger a 50p-sized piece of fresh white breadflake from dusk onwards. Use a 3 lb (1.4 kg) hook length with a size 8 hook tied direct, and wait for a slow, confident bite to develop before striking. And big rudd nearly always provide sailaway bites to big baits.

RUFFE

(Gymnocephalus cernua)

HABITAT
The ruffe is a shoal fish that likes deep rivers where currents are gentle. It often frequents the swims that are preferred by roach and gudgeon – slow mill-pools, lock cuttings, shaded spots, where trees overhang.

DISTRIBUTION
The species is absent from Ireland, Scotland and Wales. It is restricted to certain river systems in England.

PHYSICAL CHARACTERISTICS
Overall, the ruffe is rather drab in colour, completely lacking the scarlet tones of the perch, although it is perch-like in shape. All the fins are transparent grey and heavily flecked with brown markings. It has two dorsal fins, which are joined together (those of the perch are separated). The first is spiked, the second of soft rays. It also has sharp spines on the gill plates.

The back is grey-brown and irregularly speckled in dark blotches. These continue along the flanks, which often show a touch of olive. The belly is a dirty white.

REPRODUCTION
Spawning takes place usually during April, and the eggs are laid in strips among fibrous tree roots and branches or weeds in the margins. The fry hatch within 10-12 days and feed initially on microscopic plankton.

FEEDING
Adult ruffe consume all kinds of aquatic insect larvae, worms and shrimps, and the eggs and fry of other species.

FISHING FOR RUFFE
Most anglers try to avoid ruffe, and only the match fishermen or small boys will deliberately set out to catch them. They are such aggressive feeders that small animal baits such as worms, maggots and casters presented close to or on the river bed, and intended for larger species, are often gobbled up by ruffe before anything else has a chance. Indeed, when it becomes apparent that a particular spot contains a large shoal of ruffe, it is wise to change position. When absolutely nothing else is available, ruffe can be used as livebait for perch and pike.

A perch-like shape with a double (joined) dorsal fin, the ruffe is distinguished by olive flanks overlaid with dark flecks. The dorsal and tail are heavily flecked and there are spines on the gill plate.

EUROPEAN NAMES			
FRANCE	**Gremille**	ITALY	**Acernia**
GERMANY	**Kaulbarsh**	SWEDEN	**Gars**
HOLLAND	**Pos**	DENMARK	**Gers**

WEIGHT RANGE
Average size:	**3-5 in (7.5-12.5 cm)**
Record ruffe:	**5½ oz (148 g) caught by R. J. Jenkins, West View Farm, Cumbria, 1980.**

SALMON

(Salmo salar)

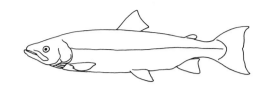

HABITAT

The salmon is a far-travelling species of the North Atlantic ocean, feeding on shoals of herring and sprats. It will tolerate only pollution-free water when it enters fresh water (usually the river of its birth) on its upriver migration to reproduce. It often travels many miles up into the tiniest of fast-water streams, resting in pools, behind boulders and other choice lies in low-water conditions along the way, and travelling fast after heavy rains.

DISTRIBUTION

The largest runs of salmon enter Irish and Scottish rivers, but several Welsh rivers enjoy good runs – the Wye in particular. In the south of England, the Avon and Test in Hampshire and the rivers of Devon have by far the most prolific runs. Owing to a re-introduction programme, the River Thames now has a modest run.

PHYSICAL CHARACTERISTICS

The salmon has a powerful, elongated, trout-like body with a large, slightly concave tail and a narrow tail root, commonly referred to as the wrist. Because the outer edges of the tail fin are rigid, this enables only the salmon to be picked out by hand or with a 'tailer'. This is one distinguishing feature that helps separate the salmon from the seatrout, which has a squared tail with soft outer edges and noticeably thicker tail root, making it almost impossible to grip tightly by hand. If you cannot easily and tightly grip the salmon around the tail root and lift, then it is a seatrout.

When fresh from the sea, the salmon's colouring is a metallic steel blue-grey along the back, fusing into sides of burnished silver, liberally flecked with small, dark, asterisk-like blotches, most of which are above the lateral line. By comparison, the sea-trout invariably has many more spots, which reach way below the lateral line – down to the pectoral root and horizontally across the entire flank.

The salmon's overall colouring darkens noticeably when it prepares for spawning. The fins and

EUROPEAN NAMES			
FRANCE	**Saumon**	SWEDEN	**Lax**
GERMANY	**Lachs**	DENMARK	**Laxs**
HOLLAND	**Zalm**	SPAIN	**Salmon**
ITALY	**Salmone**		
	Atlantico		

WEIGHT RANGE

Average size:	**6-12 lb (2.7-5.45 kg)**
Specimen size:	**Over 20 lb (9 kg)**
Record salmon:	**64 lb (29.029 kg) caught by Miss G. W. Ballantine, River Tay, Scotland, 1922.**

head darken considerably, and the body becomes a dirty grey-bronze, often with large red and brown spots appearing along the flanks. The males develop a hooked lower jaw, called a 'kype', and become most aggressive.

REPRODUCTION

While salmon enter some rivers throughout the entire calender year, spring and late summer runs are most common. Spawning usually occurs between October and January. The fish mass on the fast, gravelly shallows, where the females cut out redds (depressions) in the gravel bottom in which to deposit their large, orange eggs. These are simultaneously fertilized by milt from the males. The female then covers the eggs with stones by flapping her tail powerfully along the bottom immediately upstream from the redd.

Incubation can take as long as three or four months (until the spring) and the salmon fry, or alevins – complete with their own yolk sac on which to feed – usually stay beneath the stones for a further month before shoaling up and feeding in earnest.

Young salmon of 3-5 in (7.5-12.5 cm) long are called parr. They are beautifully coloured, with a heavily spotted back and up to a dozen oval-

shaped, blueish spots spread along the entire lateral line with a red dot between each. As these parr mature and follow their natural urge, which is to travel downriver towards the sea and rich saltwater feeding, they silver up in readiness, and are then called smolts. Smolts that return to spawn after just one year in the sea, as most do, are called grilse. A percentage, however, may wait up to three or four years in the sea before returning to the river of their birth as fully mature salmon of specimen proportions.

After the rigours of spawning a percentage die through exhaustion, particularly among the males. However, many though still weak – and in this wasted, extremely thin condition they are called kelts – return to the sea, and come back to spawn again once their body fats are replenished.

FEEDING

Salmon start fasting when they enter fresh water to spawn and consequently do not feed until their reproductive cycle is over. Fortunately for fishermen, they grab at flies, worms and spinners as a reflex action, perhaps through aggression or territorial declaration. In the sea their staple diet consists of sprats, herrings, sand eels, prawns and shrimps.

FISHING FOR SALMON

The traditional, and many would argue the most satisfying, method of catching salmon is to cover a lie or pool with the fly. The cast is made downstream and across, and the line is mended quickly by flicking a loop upstream and over before allowing the current to sweep the fly slowly round as though it were a tiny fish battling against the current force. The rod is held high throughout, and a loop of slack line is held between reel and casting hand (as a cushion when the salmon grabs hold), giving time for the hook point to find purchase before the current pressure zings the line tight. Depending on the river width, both single and double-handed rods can be used. To cover each lie or pool effectively, start at the top and simply take a pace downstream after each cast.

Exactly the same 'covering' technique can be employed when presenting artificial lures such as Devon minnows, plugs, spinners or wobbling spoons such as the toby. As with the fly, retrieve only when the current has swung the line across and the lure starts to hang or dangle immediately downstream. An alternative and very effective method, popularized in recent years with the 'flying condom' spinner, is to cast well upstream and across, which sweeps the lure quickly across the salmon's vision in a diagonal line, giving it less time to hesitate than with the fly.

A hook baited with worms, prawns and shrimps (natural or dyed) can prove deadly, especially in heavily coloured water, and when salmon have been in the river for sometime and are simply not interested in accepting the fly. The bait can be edged along or trotted downstream beneath a chunky float, or worked and bumped along just off bottom by adding shots or a bomb tied 24 in (60 cm) above the bait on a separate link that is much weaker than the 10-15 lb (4.5-6.8 kg) reel line, so it breaks instantly should the weight snag.

Left: The salmon has a powerful, streamlined body. Fresh-run fish have a metallic blue-grey sheen with asterisk spots mostly above the lateral line. Note the in-curving tail with narrow wrist.

Above: This brace of grilse, (salmon returning to spawn after just one year in the sea) have obviously been in the river for several days and started to darken noticeably.

ALLIS SHAD

(Alosa alosa)

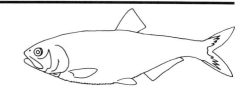

HABITAT

The allis shad spends most of its life in salt water, only entering freshwater to reproduce (see Twaite shad). Part of the reason for this particular species now being rare is that because of weir constructions across most of our major rivers which lack 'fish passes' or 'ladders', migrating upstream into clean, pure freshwater, which the allis shad must do in order to propagate its species, is virtually impossible.

DISTRIBUTION

The allis shad is a rare fish nowadays, nowhere near so commonly caught as the twaite shad, but it enters the same rivers to spawn, such as the Rivers Severn and Wye.

PHYSICAL CHARACTERISTICS

A shoaling fish with noticeably compressed sides in the herring family of fishes, to which the hard-fighting giant tarpon also belongs. In fact, the shad is almost a replica of the high-jumping tarpon, with its distinct protruding lower jaw and large hinge connecting the upper jaw. The upper jaw also has an unusual, but distinct, notch in the middle. But while the tarpon's scales are ridiculously large, those of the Allis shad are small, though quite silvery nonetheless, and easily displaced by careless handling. It is a larger, deeper-bodied (pigeon-chested) fish than the twaite shad, with a similar colour pattern of blue back and silver-golden flanks, but it usually has only one large spot on the shoulder. The Allis shad can grow to over 2 ft (60 cm) long and reach weights in excess of 8 lb (3.5 kg).

EUROPEAN NAMES			
FRANCE	**Grande Alose**	HOLLAND	**Elft**
GERMANY	**Mailfisch**	SPAIN	**La Sabogai l'alosa**

WEIGHT RANGE	
Average size:	**1½ lb (680 g)**
Specimen size:	**2½ lb (1.1 kg)**
Record allis shad:	**4 lb 12½ oz (2.166 kg) caught by P. Gerrard, Chesil Beach, Dorset, 1977.**

REPRODUCTION

It spawns higher upriver than the twaite shad, in completely fresh water, and the young may not run to sea for up to two years.

FEEDING

The allis shad consumes a planktonic diet when in the sea, plus small shoal fish.

FISHING FOR SHAD

The allis shad is now considered a threatened species and is protected under the provisions of the Wildlife and Countryside Act. (1981). It is therefore an offence to capture one intentionally. Odd individual specimens usually of between 2-4 lb (1-2 kg) are, however, taken by boat fishermen out at sea, generally on feathers and jigs.

TWAITE SHAD

(Alosa fallax)

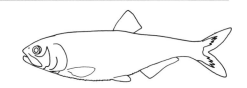

HABITAT
The twaite shad lives most of its life at sea, but it migrates each spring into fresh water, travelling upriver to spawn.

DISTRIBUTION
It is by far the more common of the two shads, but is now only really prolific around the British Isles in rivers along Ireland's west coast, and in Scotland and Wales, particularly the Wye and Severn.

PHYSICAL CHARACTERISTICS
It is a distinctly herring-like fish with a protruding bottom jaw and expanding cavernous mouth. It is covered in an even pattern of silver scales, which, like those of the herring, are easily displaced. The back is dark pewter, sometimes bluish, and there is a horizontal line of several dark spots (sometimes these are very faint) starting immediately behind the gill plate, high up on the shoulder. Strangely these spots only show up in the water. On the bank, only one or two are noticeable. The fins are weak, small in size and an even translucent grey.

REPRODUCTION
The twaite shad masses to spawn in the river's tidal reaches, usually in the vicinity of the first weir. Young shad spend up to two years in the river before running to sea.

EUROPEAN NAMES			
FRANCE	**Alose**	HOLLAND	**Fint**
	Feinte	SWEDEN	**Staksill**
GERMANY	**Finte**		

WEIGHT RANGE	
Average size:	1-1¼ lb (450-560 g)
Specimen size:	1¾-2 lb (790-900 g)
Record twaite shad:	3 lb 2 oz (1.417 kg) caught by S. Jenkins, Torbay, Devon, 1954.

FEEDING
Adults feed on sand eels, sprats and herrings, plus a quantity of plankton.

FISHING FOR SHAD
In the sea, shad are most frequently caught on small feathers, while in fresh water they provide excellent fun on a super-light spinning outfit and 4 lb (1.8 kg) test line combo. Use small, size 00 mepps-type spinners or tiny fly spoons. It is well worth trying for them with the fly rod, presenting silver-bodied imitative fish fry lures, such as zonkers or polystickles, on a sinktip or sinking line. Worms trotted beneath an Avon-type float through the fast water of weir pools where shad congregate are also effective at tempting this unique fish. It is very acrobatic, and a lively fighter.

The twaite shad has a silver, herring-like body, an even scale pattern, forked tail, and line of spots behind the gill plate, only visible in water. Out of water only one spot is noticeable.

SMELT

(Osmerus eperlanus)

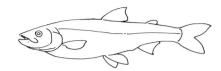

HABITAT

The smelt is a shoal fish that spends the greater part of its life in the sea around the coastline and in estuaries, only entering fresh water proper for the purpose of reproduction.

DISTRIBUTION

The species is quite localized around the British Isles, with the largest concentrations found around the east coast from the Humber down to the Thames estuary.

PHYSICAL CHARACTERISTICS

It is frequently called the cucumber smelt due to its inherent and distinct smell of cucumbers, which is quite strong even when it is dead. It has a slim, dace-like shape with a big eye and cavernous, upturned mouth containing quite large teeth. The tail is deeply forked, but the dorsal and anal fins are squared. It has a tiny adipose fin. Colouring varies from a pale, transparent grey-green along the back to flanks of metallic silver. Smelt has an unusually short lateral line starting at the gill plate.

REPRODUCTION

Smelt enter the lower tidal reaches of rivers *en masse* during the months of March and April, when spawning takes place. Their yellow, sticky eggs adhere to weeds and rocks, and the fry are taken by the tide out into the estuary.

FEEDING

The smelt's favourite food is worms, shrimps and the fry of other fish.

FISHING FOR SMELT

Although smelt are occasionally taken on maggots by anglers fishing tidal rivers for dace and roach, it is never fished for deliberately. However, due to its unusual smell, smelt is one of the most popular and effective of the deadbaits used for pike, whether it is presented static on the bottom, drifted beneath a float or wobbled.

EUROPEAN NAMES		
FRANCE	**Eperlan**	HOLLAND **Spiering**
GERMANY	**Stint**	
WEIGHT RANGE		
Average size:	**6-10 in (15-25 cm) long**	

The smelt smells of cucumbers. It has a slim, grey-green-silvery body, protruding lower jaw lined with sizeable teeth, a tiny adipose fin, large eye and forked tail.

THREE-SPINED STICKLEBACK

(Gasterosteus aculeatus)

belly in place of pelvic fins, it has a single spine. The 'second' dorsal has soft rays. It has an upturned mouth with a protruding lower jaw, thick-rimmed lips and a large eye. Colouring along the back is dark pewter, blending into flanks of yellowy-silver. Male sticklebacks (aptly called 'red-throats') colour up vividly in the spawning season, developing a red flash under the chin, bright olive green along the flanks, and a blue outer circle to the eye.

REPRODUCTION

The stickleback spawns in the late spring, when the males construct a loose-woven nest on the bottom from plant tissue. Following a courtship ritual, the male entices a female to lay her eggs in the nest, where they are immediately fertilized.

FEEDING

Sticklebacks eat worms, molluscs and aquatic insect larvae, and even prey on fish fry.

FISHING FOR STICKLEBACKS

Schoolboys catch sticklebacks with a small, thin worm tied in the middle to a length of thread, using a matchstick as a float. The fish gorge on one end of the worm and can be lifted out before they have the sense to let go.

NOTE

A closely related, but less common species is the ten- or nine-spined stickleback, the males of which have a black throat during the spawning season.

The stickleback has a bony, scale-less body with a sawn-off tail. Three spines replace the first dorsal. Males (top fish) develop a red throat and green eye when spawning. The bottom two fish pictured here are ten-spined sticklebacks.

HABITAT

The stickleback is a shoaling fish that colonizes most small ponds, pits, lakes and sluggish, stagnant rivers, including canals, ditches and dykes, even those running through purely salt marshlands.

DISTRIBUTION

The stickleback is extremely common throughout the British Isles.

PHYSICAL CHARACTERISTICS

The species is small but aggressive, and is a rather strange shape with a shiny, scale-less, bony body. It has three strong spines where its first dorsal should be, and directly beneath that, under the

EUROPEAN NAMES			
FRANCE	**Epinoch**	HOLLAND	**Stekelbaars**
GERMANY	**Stichling**	SWEDEN	**Storspigg**

WEIGHT RANGE	
Average size:	1½-2½ in (3.75-6.25 cm) long

TENCH

(Tinca tinca)

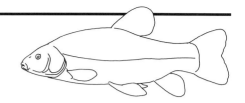

HABITAT

Although present in many sluggish river systems and canals, and even rivers of moderate pace, tench much prefer a quiet life and grow fattest in stillwaters. Rich, clear-water, weedy estate lakes and nicely matured old gravel and sand pits where the thick layers of accumulated silt attract massive colonies of bloodworm (midge larvae) breed tench both in numbers and of an exceptionally large average size. As long as the food chain is not dominated by competition species, such as an unusually high bream or carp population, tench also fair well in small, man-made ponds and lakes, in reservoirs and in weedy irrigation channels or drains.

Tench are rarely far from cover and love to browse through beds of lilies, Canadian pondweed and hornwort, sipping in aquatic insects. They also work along the edge of sedge and rush beds and through dense beds of tall common reed, the tops of which can be seen 'knocking' as tench pick off food items such as caddis grubs, and snails and their eggs, clinging to the fibrous stems close to the bottom. Tench also frequent deep troughs, holes and gullies in large gravel pits, often following a regular daily 'feeding' route.

DISTRIBUTION

Tench are present in the majority of lakes, meres, broads, gravel-pit complexes and reservoirs throughout England, and in many river and canal systems throughout Ireland, England and much of Wales, but are comparatively rare in Scotland.

PHYSICAL CHARACTERISTICS

The tench is a slow, ponderous species, purpose-built for grubbing about on the bottom. It has rounded, thick-set features and large fins coloured quite evenly in dark grey-brown.

The easiest way of distinguishing between males and females is to look at the pelvic fins of each. Those of the male, which are large, spoon-shaped and rather crinkly, overlap the vent when smoothed against the belly, while the female's pel-

vics are pointed, much smaller and do not overlap the vent. The eye is red, the mouth semi-protrusible and slightly upturned with thick-rimmed lips. At each corner of the mouth is the tiniest of barbels. Even the tench's overall colouring of olive green is unique, and instantly eliminates the possibility of confusion with any other British freshwater species. The scales are tiny, deeply embedded and covered in a thick, gel-like mucus, which is reputed to have healing properties for any ailing fish that rubs up alongside (hence its nickname 'doctor fish').

REPRODUCTION

In a warm spring, tench can be seen chasing each other about over the weedy shallows in preparation for spawning at the end of May or in June, although following a cold spring they could hold back until July. The female spreads her eggs over soft, rooted plants or through dense marginal grasses, reed and rush beds. She is often accompanied by up to several eager males, which spray milt over the eggs to ensure fertilization. Fry take 6-10 days to hatch and remain in thick cover, feeding first on microscopic plankton and then on aquatic insects until they are several inches long. These small fish are seldom caught on rod and line.

EUROPEAN NAMES			
FRANCE	Tanche	SWEDEN	Sutare
GERMANY	Schleie	DENMARK	Suder
HOLLAND	Zeelt	SPAIN	Tenca
ITALY	Tinca		

WEIGHT RANGE	
Average size:	2-3 lb (900 g-1.35 kg)
Specimen size:	Over 5 lb (2.25 kg)
Record tench:	14 lb 3 oz (6.435 kg) caught by P. A. Gooriah, Wraysbury No. One Pit, Middx, 1987.

FEEDING

Tench have the strange habit of standing on their heads to suck up food from the bottom detritus. They emit tiny, tell-tale bubbles, which escape through their gill filaments during chewing. These rise to the surface along with natural gas bubbles from the disturbed sediment, pinpointing the presence of feeding below.

In addition to syphoning up bloodworms and annelid worms from the silt, tench eat crustacea – including shrimps – water lice, large zooplankton such as daphnia, plus numerous molluscs from snails to pea-shell cockles. They also consume all forms of aquatic insect larvae.

FISHING FOR TENCH

For close-range situations among gaps between

A rounded, distinct olive-green body, dark grey fins and a tiny red eye. Male tench (right) have spoon-shaped pelvics which cover the vent.

lilies, between dense weedbeds and in deep, marginal swims, tench are most effectively caught by floatfishing. Use the lift method with the bottom shot just 3-4 in (7.5-10 cm) from the bait, so that the float tip rises when the tench sucks it up. In weedy, snaggy areas, tench readily accept large, freelined offerings such as the entire insides of a swan mussel, a big lobworm, cube of luncheon meat or trout pellet paste.

To present the bait to tench inhabiting distant swims, use an open-end swimfeeder rig. Use breadcrumbs as the attractor, with casters, sweetcorn, brandlings, or maggots on the hook.

A bobbin or monkey-climber indicator used in conjunction with an electric bite alarm provides perfect visual/audible indication.

Where carp share a fishery with tench, tench soon learn to accept even large boilies as part of their natural food, so offer mini or medium-sized boilies on a ledger set-up, and loosefeed with the same.

GOLDEN TENCH

Identical in shape to the tench, although it rarely attains weights in excess of 3 lb (1.35 kg), the rare golden tench has a bright yellowy body, often indiscriminately flecked with dark blotches. Its fins are translucent with a pinkish tinge, and it has an unmistakeable jet black eye.

Golden tench have a bright orange-yellow body, sometimes marked with dark flecks. Fins have a distinct pinkish tinge and the eye is jet black.

AMERICAN BROOK TROUT

(Salvelinus fontinalis)

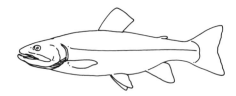

HABITAT
In Canada and the USA, from where it originates, this fish is called brook charr, and lives in the cold, pure water of streams, rivers and lakes.

DISTRIBUTION
In the hope of providing more varied fly fishing, brook trout were stocked into numerous stillwater fisheries, mostly in the south of England, throughout the 1970s and 1980s. However, because of the extra cost of rearing them in comparatively small numbers, and the fact that they tend to group or shoal up and not move freely around the fishery – as rainbows do – few waters in the British Isles are now stocked with brook trout.

PHYSICAL CHARACTERISTICS
In overall shape and thickness, the 'brookie' is similar to the brown trout, but rather stockier. It has very small scales and charr-like, mosaic markings along the back and flanks – small, irregular-shaped, cream spots on a pewter-grey background. The belly is silver-white. The pectoral, pelvic and anal fins have a distinctive, unmistakable, charr-like white edging with an inner black line.

REPRODUCTION
When stocked in to British waters, 'brookies' rarely breed in the wild. They are bred and reared almost entirely by fish farmers, primarily in the south of England.

FEEDING
The brook trout consumes all manner of aquatic insects, shrimps, molluscs and small fishes.

FISHING FOR AMERICAN BROOK TROUT
Most methods used for tempting brown and rainbow trout with artificial nymphs and wet flies in man-made fisheries will also catch American Brook trout. For further tips, see Brown trout and Rainbow trout.

With a deep-bodied, typical trout shape, the American brook trout has very small scales, charr-like flanks of cream spots on pewter-grey, and a white edge to the pectoral, pelvic and anal fins.

EUROPEAN NAMES

FRANCE	Saumon de fontaine	ITALY	Salmerino di torrente
GERMANY	Bachsaibling	SWEDEN	Amerikansk bekkerøye
HOLLAND	Bronfovel	DENMARK	Kildeørred

WEIGHT RANGE

Average size:	1-2 lb (450-900 g)
Specimen size:	Over 3 lb (1.35 kg)
Record American brook trout:	5 lb 13½ oz (2.650 kg) caught by A. Pearson, Avington Fishery, Hampshire, 1981.

BROWN TROUT

(Salmo trutta)

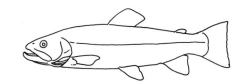

HABITAT

Like all salmonids, the brown trout demands clean, pure, unpolluted water in brooks, streams, rivers, lakes, lochs and reservoirs, and is thus an excellent barometer of water quality. In rivers it occupies the fast, shallow, well-oxygenated stretches, and loves feature lies behind boulders, bridge supports, weedrafts and overhangs, where it can move out to intercept food items brought downstream by the current. In stillwaters, it generally prefers deeper areas than, for instance, the rainbow trout.

DISTRIBUTION

The species is common throughout the British Isles in all clear-flowing streams, rivers and lochs, and in countless man-made lakes and reservoirs where they have been introduced for the sole purpose of fly fishing.

PHYSICAL CHARACTERISTICS

While the brown trout, even to the layman, is perhaps the most easily recognizable of all freshwater fish, it varies enormously in colouring from one type of environment to another. Those from peaty-coloured burns, for instance, could be bronze along the back and flanks, with a mixture of red and black spots (some with an outer ring of white) that cover the entire flank way below the lateral line. Brown trout from chalkstreams may also have white rings around extremely large red, black or brown spots and a distinctly buttery-yellow belly.

In complete contrast, brown trout inhabiting deep, clear-water reservoirs may have bright silver sides with dark, very much smaller, 'asterisk-type' spots and a silver-white belly. In truth, a brown trout could, and often does, look like dozens of entirely different species of trout.

In overall shape the brown trout has more rounded features than the salmon, with a noticeably thick tail root, the tail itself being either squared or slightly concave. Adult males have a curved lower jaw, which becomes more pro-

EUROPEAN NAMES			
FRANCE	**Truite**	SWEDEN	**Bäcköring**
GERMANY	**Bachforelle**	DENMARK	**Baekørred**
HOLLAND	**Beekforel**	SPAIN	**Trutta**
ITALY	**Trotta**		

WEIGHT RANGE

Average size:	**1-2 lb/mere ounces in tiny streams (450-900 g)**
Specimen size:	**over 5 lb**
Record brown trout:	**cultivated – 20 lb 3¾ oz (9.178 kg) caught by J. Gardner, Dever Springs, 1991; wild – 19 lb 10½ oz (8.923 kg) caught by A. Thorne, Pitlochry, 1993.**

nounced during the spawning season.

REPRODUCTION

The brown trout spawns in the exceptionally shallow water of tributaries and sidestreams or carriers during the winter months – between October and January – the female depositing her large eggs into a shallow redd (depression) cut in the gravel. These are simultaneously fertilized with milt from the cock fish, and the offspring develop through the alevin, fry and parr stages, as do all salmonids.

FEEDING

This species has extremely catholic tastes. It gobbles up almost anything edible, including all forms and stages of aquatic insect life, crustacea, molluscs, small fish – including the eggs, fry and parr of other salmonids – worms, and anglers' baits such as bread, maggots and sweetcorn.

FISHING FOR TROUT

River trout easily fall to the upstream worm, and to one presented downstream with the current, either freelined or trotted beneath a chunky float. They

Chris Turnbull 93

also accept stationary baits ledgered on the bottom. In addition they snap up small spoons and spinners, and small livebaits such as gudgeon, bullheads, loach or minnows presented beneath a float. However, most stocked fisheries have a fly-only rule (to protect the brown trout from its own greed), which provides a much greater challenge.

The dry fly is considered the most sporting method of all. Next comes the nymph presented upstream just like the dry fly, with part of the cast de-greased to let the artificial (which can be a leaded pattern to overcome fast, or deep runs) work naturally at the depth at which trout are holding. Before weed becomes troublesome in the

Here is the classic trout shape. The brown trout has variable colour along its flanks from silver to bronze, and can have black, brown or red spots ringed in white. It has a silver or yellow belly and a thick tail root.

summer, the wet fly presented in the traditional manner – downstream and across – really scores, especially in fast or turbulent pools.

In large stillwaters such as lochs and reservoirs, the most effective method is loch-style fishing from a slowly drifting boat (using a drogue to reduce the boat's speed in strong winds), casting a team of flies directly downwind. To reach the monster brown trout that stay deep in reservoirs, use a fast-sinking line and fish-imitating flies fully 5 in (12.5 cm) long. The massive brown trout of deep lochs (often called 'ferox') are caught by trolling, using large spoons either flat-line or presented on a downrigger unit.

On large, windswept lakes, dapping – making a large, bushy fly or a live insect such as a grasshopper dance enticingly on the water – is a deadly method, much used in Ireland: a length of floss is incorporated into the cast to catch the wind.

TROUT HYBRIDS

During the 1970s-1980s, fish farmers in southern England, such as the famous Avington and Nythe Lake fisheries in Hampshire, specialized in selective breeding and the stocking of hybrid trout. It was an exciting, rather fashionable, but costly exercise that fizzled out because the hybrids fought and tasted no better than the species from which they were derived.

TIGER TROUT

The tiger (or zebra) trout is a cross between the American brook trout and the brown trout. It has beautiful, squiggly, gold markings over a deep bronze body, with a golden yellow belly. Its pectoral, pelvic and anal fins are edged in white like those of its male parent, the brook trout.

A cross between an American brook trout and the brown trout, the tiger trout has squiggly, irregular-shaped gold markings over a bronze-grey body. The lower fins have white edges.

CHEETAH TROUT

The cheetah trout is the result of cross-breeding rainbow trout with an American brook trout. This produces a stocky, most unusually coloured hybrid that retains a suggestion of the pinky-magenta hue of the rainbow along its flanks, overlaid with irregular-shaped spots and wavy markings. Its pectoral, pelvic and anal fins also have the white edging of the 'brookie'.

BROWNBOW

The brownbow is exactly what its name implies: the hybrid from crossing brown trout with rainbow trout. This was a common practice some years

back, but is now rarely done because the resulting hybrids were neither as strong nor as durable as either parent.

A fast-growing and sexless, deep-bodied rainbow trout. Bright silver sides have only a hint of magenta; the triploid trout is heavily spotted.

TRIPLOID

The triploid is a rainbow trout reared from fertilized eggs that have been subjected to immersion in hot water. This sudden 'shock' produces a beautiful, silver-bodied sexless rainbow that uses all its energy to pack on weight extremely fast – in contrast to a hen fish, which produces eggs and becomes eggbound, and a cock fish, which darkens up and attacks others at spawning time.

During the production of triploids, however, there can be massive egg losses. In addition, there is no guarantee that all those reared on are, in fact, sexless rainbows, and it is not possible to tell until they are over 1 lb (450 g) in weight. For these reasons, only a limited number of fisheries stock with triploid trout.

Fish farms in Scotland that specialize in rearing salmon triploids for the table have enjoyed a greater level of success by treating the fertilized eggs to 'pressure' rather than heat. However, this method is not nearly so successful with trout.

RAINBOW TROUT

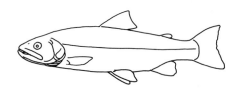

(Salmo gairderi)

HABITAT

Although the rainbow prefers relatively cold water (like other salmonids), it has a much greater tolerance than the brown trout of warm, less well-oxygenated, small man-made fisheries, be they excavated from peat, chalk, or sand and gravel seams. For this reason, plus the fact that it repeatedly jumps and puts up a fast, exciting fight, and is not difficult to tempt on the fly, it is by far the most widely caught trout of all in both rivers and stillwaters.

DISTRIBUTION

The rainbow reproduces in the wild in only a few locations within the British Isles. However, most modern fly fisheries – from the chalkstreams of Berkshire, to pit and lake stillwaters of just a few acres, to the mighty Rutland Reservoir (the largest

The rainbow trout has the classical trout shape, a rounded head, and is heavily spotted over entire body (except the belly), dorsal and tail. It has a streak of pink-magenta over the gill plate and sometimes along the entire flank.

EUROPEAN NAMES

FRANCE	Truite arc-en-ciel	ITALY	Trota Iridia
		SWEDEN	Regnbage
GERMANY	Regen-bogen forelle	DENMARK	Regn-bureørred
		SPAIN	Trucha Arco-iris
HOLLAND	Regenboog forell		

WEIGHT RANGE

Average size:	1-4 lb (450 g-1.8 kg)
Specimen size:	Over 10 lb (4.5 kg)
Record rainbow trout:	29 lb 12 oz (13.506 kg) caught by A. McIntyre, Lock Tay, 1993.

man-made lake in Europe) – stock far more heavily with rainbow than brown trout.

PHYSICAL CHARACTERISTICS

The rainbow is aggressive, and exceptionally swift and acrobatic in its movements. It has the classic trout shape, but is noticeably more rounded across the snout than 'brownies' and sea trout. An unmistakable pink-to-magenta flash runs along the flanks and gill plate, although some fish, especially reservoir rainbows – well-conditioned hens in particular – can look like the proverbial 'bar of silver', with not the slightest trace of purple. The back is usually an olive-pewter heavily dotted with small, dark spots, which also cover the flanks to a line level with the pectoral fins and even the tail, which is slightly concave. The belly is usually silvery white. The rainbow is by far the most densely spotted of all trout, and by this fact alone is easily distinguished from all others. Males tend to colour up more and have a slightly protruding lower jaw.

REPRODUCTION

Within the British Isles rainbow trout are almost entirely fish-farm bred. Although reproduction occurs in isolated rivers where conditions suit, this is uncommon. In the wild their spawning cycle occurs between January and May on the stony shallows of streams and carriers to the main river. The large, orange eggs are deposited in a redd (depression) excavated from the gravel bottom by the female's tail, and they are simultaneously fertilized by milt from the cock fish, which darkens considerably in colour during spawning.

FEEDING

The rainbow enjoys a varied diet, including all stages of aquatic insect life, terrestrial flies that land on the water, shrimps, snails and small fish such as loach, bullheads, minnows and sticklebacks. They also quickly gobble up baits such as worms, bread and maggots intended for coarse species.

FISHING FOR RAINBOW TROUT

In rivers, both the upstream nymph and the dry fly are the most enjoyable methods for tempting rainbows, which rise freely. When fishing in stillwaters, however, particularly when there is little hatching fly life to imitate, slow-sinking leaded shrimps or nymphs (on size 14-8 hooks) can prove deadly. In crystal-clear water, try stealthily stalking an individual fish – either stationary or on patrol – by accurately placing the artificial to free-fall ahead of the trout and then making an erratic retrieve to make it simulate a live creature. This can induce a take, and it is often possible to observe the rainbow inhaling the artificial. In lakes and reservoirs where boat fishing is permitted, loch-style fly fishing with a team of flies – two wet and one dry (the bob fly) on sizes 14 and 12 hooks – is a most exciting method whenever there is a good ripple on. Aim to place the flies immediately downwind into the 'slicks' or wind lanes along which rainbows hunt for food. In the cold water of the early season, use large black, orange or white lures on size 8 hooks and fish deep with a sunken line, retrieving very slowly.

In mental terms the most effective way of coming to grips with huge, seemingly featureless waters such as lochs, and especially the massive man-made reservoirs created by flooding entire valleys in which rainbows are nowadays regularly stocked, is literally to think of the habitat in cross section, like a layer cake. This helps put these deep waters in perspective, because only very rarely will the rainbow trout occupy all water layers between the surface and the bottom. And as some reservoirs contain vast areas of water from 30 down to 100 feet (9-30 m) deep, anticipating or locating the 'taking' depth through trial and error is imperative. In really sunny, flat, calm conditions for instance, rainbows are reknowned for going deep into colder layers, while in windy, cool conditions, when the surface is nicely broken, they might confidently feed all day in the upper layers close to the surface.

SEA TROUT

(Salmo trutta trutta)

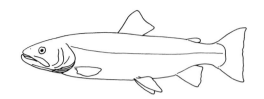

HABITAT

Although it belongs to the same species as the brown trout, the sea trout spends the greater part of its life at sea, entering fresh water only for the purpose of reproduction. Like the salmon, it migrates only into pure, fast-flowing rivers, travelling far inland into the high upper reaches, often via lochs. It does not, however, generally make the long pilgrimage to distant feeding grounds like the salmon, preferring to stay in territorial coastal waters.

DISTRIBUTION

Sea trout enter all clean, unpolluted river systems around the British Isles as early as April and as late as the end of September. Rivers along the west

EUROPEAN NAMES

FRANCE	Truite de Mer	SWEDEN	Havs-laxöring
GERMANY	Meerforelle	DENMARK	Havørred
HOLLAND	Zeeforel	SPAIN	Trutta Marina
ITALY	Trotta di Mare		

WEIGHT RANGE

Average size: **1-2 lb (450-900 g)**
Specimen size: **Over 6-7 lb (2.7-3.1 kg)**
Record sea trout: **28 lb 5¼ oz (12.850 kg) caught by J. Farrant, estuary of River Test, Hampshire, 1992.**

coast of Ireland and Scotland and those along the coastline of Wales enjoy by far the strongest runs.

PHYSICAL CHARACTERISTICS

When they have been in the river for some time, adult sea trout darken considerably and look very much like brown trout (which, of course, they are – but a migrant form), except for a lack of red spots. Numerous varying strains of sea trout have evolved, and it is nothing out of the ordinary to catch two very different-looking sea trout from the same river, which makes accurate identification rather confusing.

When fresh from the sea, however – complete with sea lice – sea trout are noticeably streamlined. They have a metallic pewter sheen liberally spotted with small, dark asterisks; and the proverbial 'bar

of silver' just like the salmon, which can also make identification difficult.

While young sea trout may have a slightly forked tail, that of the adult is squared or even slightly convex. The salmon's tail, by comparison, is always concave or slightly forked, and narrow at the root or 'wrist' with rigid outer edges, enabling it to be easily gripped and lifted (see Salmon). The salmon's spots are usually confined to its shoulders and upper flank above the lateral line, while those of the sea trout are usually far more numerous (but not always), and cover the flank down to a line level with the pectoral root. In addition, the sea trout's anal fin, which is more pointed than that of the salmon, has an outer leading edge that is longer than the inner one, even when it is pressed against the body.

REPRODUCTION
Sea trout spawn sometime between October and December in shallow, fast parts of the upper river, in narrow tributaries and streams, where the water is high in dissolved oxygen and the bottom coarse gravel. Also, like other salmonids, infant sea trout develop through the alevin, fry and parr stages (see Salmon), remaining in the river for two to three years before silvering up and running to sea – when they are called smolts. A percentage return after just a few months in saltwater, but the majority return the following year to spawn.

FEEDING
When returning to fresh water for the sole purpose of spawning, adult sea trout fast, just like salmon, but lesser fish will gorge on salmonid eggs, min-nows, fry and the young parr of all trouts, in addition to aquatic insect life and the worm or maggot baits of coarse fishermen, particularly in the lower and tidal river stretches.

FISHING FOR SEA TROUT
When trying to catch sea trout that have been in the river for a while, resting in pools during their upstream migration while waiting for a push of water, fly fishing at night is the method, especially in really clear, low water. Very early morning and dusk are also recommended. No small degree of stealth is needed as sea trout are the most wary of all salmonids. In addition to single-hook, standard wet-fly patterns, tandem lures and treble-hook tube flies will catch them. In still conditions, the wake of a surface lure will sometimes tempt one to grab hold, particularly in clear water after dark.

Sea trout in lochs or loughs can be taken from a boat by drift-fishing downwind, and they will accept both the point and bob fly. Spinning from the bank, or from the sea shore at the mouth of an estuary during the summer months, when the greatest runs occur, can also be productive. Use small bar spoons or mepps-type spinners in sizes 1-3. Worming as for salmon also catches sea trout (see Salmon) when searching in rivers. Explore all the pools methodically.

Right: The sea trout has a streamlined, classical game fish shape with a metallic pewter sheen when fresh run. It is heavily spotted, usually over the entire flanks. Adults have a squared tail and a thick tail root.
Below: Favourite artificials for catching seatrout in estuaries and in the sea proper, are toby lures and flying condoms.

THE WHITEFISH

POWAN *(Coregonus lavaretus)*

VENDACE *(Coregonus albula)*

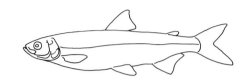

EUROPEAN NAMES (POWAN)			
FRANCE	**Bondelle**	SWEDEN	**Sik**
GERMANY	**Schnapel**		

EUROPEAN NAMES (VENDACE)			
FRANCE	**Petite Marêne**	GERMANY	**Kleine**
		SWEDEN	**Sikoja**

WEIGHT RANGE

(Applies to both species)

Average size:	6-10 in (15-25 cm)
Specimen size:	Over 12 oz (55 g)
Record powan:	2 lb 1½ oz (950 g) caught by S. M. Barrie, Haweswater Reservoir. Cumbria, 1986.

HABITAT
The whitefish is a shoal fish that inhabits deep, cold, clear-water lakes and lochs.

DISTRIBUTION
Isolated populations exist in deep Welsh lakes (Lake Bala), in the Lake District, in the Scottish lochs and Irish loughs.

PHYSICAL CHARACTERISTICS
For many decades, both scientists and fishermen alike assumed there were numerous separate species of whitefish within the British Isles – fish with strange names like houting, powan, pollan, vendace, gwyniad, schelly and skelly. It is now generally accepted, however (although not by everyone), that these herring-like survivors of a bygone age could simply be just two separate species, the vendace and the powan, which, having been locked up in a time warp since the last Ice Age, have evolved with slight physical variations particular to their individual environments. While

both have an even-scaled, silver body with a tiny adipose fin like grayling and trout, there is one easy way of separating powan from vendace. The powan has a slightly protruding top lip, while the vendace has a protruding, herring-like lower jaw. The vendace also has a large eye and slimmer body.

As the whitefish have been included on the endangered species list and are protected under the provisions of the Wildlife and Countryside Act (1981), their exact identification is rather academic because it is now an offence to catch them intentionally.

REPRODUCTION

Whitefish spawn between December and February, depositing their eggs in the gravel bottom.

FEEDING

They consume plankton, molluscs and aquatic insect larvae, and very occasionally the eggs and tiny fry of other species.

FISHING FOR WHITEFISH

It is now an offence to fish for whitefish, although the occasional one sucks in small worms or maggots intended for coarse species and the small imitative patterns of the fly fisherman. In the deep, cold lakes of central Europe, whitefish are most successfully caught on teams of tiny buzzer-like flies just above the bottom, bumped gently along with a small bomb.

The powan has a long, slim, silver body, a forked tail, even scale pattern, adipose fin, and a slightly protruding top jaw. The vendace has a protruding lower jaw.

ZANDER

(Stizostedion lucioperca)

HABITAT

Zander usually prefer to occupy the deepest and darkest channels and pools in both lake and river systems. Natural holes and depressions along the bottom where side drains or ditches converge with the main flow, and confluences where a secondary river or stream enters, are much favoured zander hotspots.

Areas that become coloured due to an injection of flood water also hold enormous attraction for zander. Dark, deep gullies beneath road and rail bridges, weir- and mill-ponds, boat basins – all also attract resident zander shoals if the system contains them.

DISTRIBUTION

Within the British Isles, zander are present only in England. They are, in fact, slowly spreading throughout the south and Midlands following their controversial introduction during the early 1960s into the Great Ouse relief channel at Downham Market, Norfolk, but shoals are still comparatively isolated.

They have, however, become prolific within the entire Fenland system of interconnecting drainage channels and rivers in Cambridgeshire, Lincolnshire and Norfolk.

Zander have also been stocked into numerous stillwater fisheries throughout England, and have even found their way (illegally, of course) into other river systems far from the fens.

PHYSICAL CHARACTERISTICS

Some people call zander pike-perch, and while it may very well resemble both of these species, the zander has, in fact, been uniquely designed and is exceptionally well equipped for preying upon small cyprinid shoal fish, plus, of course, its own young.

The body is long, slim and covered in very rough scales. Colouring is blueish-grey along the back, fusing into metallic brassy-pewter below the distinct lateral line. There are several vertical blueish bars reaching down to the lateral line, although these are often more evident on zander inhabiting clear water.

The zander's most noticeable feature is its fins. All are large, especially the dorsal, which is split into two, the first consisting of strong spines, and the second of soft, branched rays. Both are translucent grey and flecked with dark blotches, as is the large forked tail. The pectoral, pelvic and anal fins are a pale translucent grey that sometimes has a warm tinge.

The zander has a comparatively small head with strong jaws containing a real armoury of needle-sharp teeth. Set into the front of the jaw are four large canines used for instantly immobilizing the unfortunate prey. The eyes are rather glassy-looking and very large, providing the zander with tremendous vision and the ability to hunt during the hours of darkness and in heavily coloured water.

REPRODUCTION

Spawning takes place in the early spring in shallow water, and the eggs are distributed around reed and rush stems or over a gravel bottom, where the fry hatch some two weeks later. Initially, the fry feed on zooplankton and other crustacea before

EUROPEAN NAMES			
FRANCE	Sandre	SWEDEN	Gös
GERMANY	Zander	DENMARK	Sandart
HOLLAND	Sanner		
ITALY	Lucioperca o sandra		

WEIGHT RANGE	
Average size:	2-5 lb (900 g-2.25 kg)
Specimen size:	8-9 lb (3.6-4.1 kg) plus
Record zander:	18 lb 10 oz (8.460 kg) caught by R. Armstrong, River Severn, 1993.

aspiring to a mainly predatory diet of small fish as they mature. Like perch, zander shoal in large groups or year classes, which slowly diminish in numbers. Large, adult zander are often solitary or part of a very small group.

FEEDING

Zander hunt in packs, usually close to the bottom. They feed more actively in low light levels at dawn, dusk and particularly during the hours of darkness, when their vision is superior to that of their prey – small shoal fish such as rudd, dace, roach and bream.

Zander also eat perch, and prey heavily on their own young. As a 2-3 in (5-7.5 cm) section of freshwater eel is a most effective zander bait, it is only natural to assume that they also prey on eels – which, of course, are more active during darkness.

Zander respond quickly to changes in light values during daylight hours, and may be triggered into a feeding spree when a bright day suddenly turns overcast, or vice versa.

FISHING FOR ZANDER

Occasionally zander suck up a bunch of maggots or worms intended for other species, but generally speaking, zander are looking for small fish to eat. Therefore, floatfished small livebaits presented free-roaming, and particularly on a paternoster float rig set so that the bait works only 2 ft (60 cm) above bottom, are the most effective. Ledgered livebaits work well, too.

In heavily coloured waters or in clear water during darkness, a small, freshly killed deadbait, such as a 3-4 in (7.5-10 cm) roach or rudd, has enormous attraction. Pierce the flank several times to allow the bait's aroma to permeate the surrounding water. Use a 10 lb (4.5 kg) wire trace holding a duo of size 10 semi-barbless trebles.

Zander also respond to small jigs/spinners. Two zander look-alikes on the other side of the Atlantic, the sauger and walleye, are more commonly caught with small artificials.

The best daytime conditions are during strong winds, at dawn and dusk, and at night during the summer, autumn and in bouts of mild winter weather. Zander are difficult to locate in sub-zero conditions.

Zander feed on a mainly predatory diet of small fish and hunt more actively in low light levels at dawn, dusk, and particularly during the hours of darkness.

Chris Turnbull 93

WALLEYE (PIKE-PERCH)
(Stizostedion vitreum)

This North American close cousin of the zander was stocked into isolated fisheries several decades ago and is now either extinct or has interbred with zander. The record weighed 11 lb 12 oz (5 kg 329 g) and was caught by F. Adams from The Delph at Welney, Norfolk, in 1934.

The zander has very large fins with two dorsals. It has a small head, strong teeth, a glassy eye, brassy-pewter flanks, which are sometimes barred, and rough skin.

128